The Complete Photo Guide to

BEADING

Creative Publishing
international

First published in the United States of America by
Creative Publishing international, Inc., a member of
Quayside Publishing Group
400 First Avenue North
Suite 300
Minneapolis, MN 55401
1-800-328-3895
www.creativepub.com

ISBN: 978-1-58923-718-6

10 9 8 7 6 5 4 3 2 1

Library of Congress Cataloging-in-Publication Data available

Copy Editor: Catherine Broberg
Proofreader: Ellen Goldstein
Book and Cover Design: Kim Winscher
Page Layout: Laurie Young
Photographs: Robin Atkins and
Creative Publishing international

Printed in China.

The Complete Photo Guide to
BEADING

Creative Publishing
international

CONTENTS

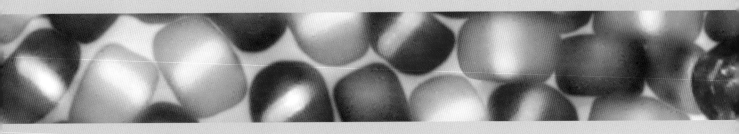

Introduction

THE MAGIC OF BEADS

Have you ever held a few beads in your hands and wondered at the magic and mystery of their journey, about who made them, and where they came from? Small, beautiful, intriguing, and infinitely varied, beads are so compelling that people sometimes buy them without a clue about what to do with them.

Whether you already own a stash of beads or possess none at all, this book will teach—and show—you many different ways to use beads without having to acquire expensive equipment or materials. Those with no beading experience will find everything they need to begin learning techniques and creating bead jewelry and other beaded objects. Those with experience in one or more types of beading will find areas where they can expand and enhance their skills.

At the most fundamental level, there are three types of things you can do with beads: string, weave, or embroider. This book covers all three categories. Within each category, you will find a variety of techniques shown through a broad range of projects. You'll learn all the basics, including design ideas, techniques, and tips for creating various objects with beads—some to wear, some to give away, some to decorate your home, and some just for fun.

THE SAGA OF BEADS

Some anthropologists believe that beads are human's earliest artifacts, predating tools and vessels. Whatever the exact time line, we know that early humans pierced natural materials like bone and shell, stringing them on grass or reeds to make personal adornments.

In nearly every culture and every land since the very beginning, people have found ways to make and use beads. From primitive cultures to the ruling classes, from earliest humans to modern times, beads are nearly ubiquitous.

In the past few centuries, beading was considered a craft. Although some types of beading required great skill, such as the beaded handbags created by Victorian women, and some crafters of beaded jewelry attained position and status, beads and beading were largely ignored in the art world. However, in recent years, many people have begun to view beading as an art as well as a craft. Increasing numbers of beaders are considered artists, their beadwork recognized by collectors, museums, and galleries as an important art form.

Small, easily portable, often used in barter or trade, beads are given value based on their age, uniqueness, and the material from which they are made. Since most types of beads are durable, they can last for hundreds of years, passing from hand to hand, being repurposed and relocated by each owner. The history and future of beads (and beaded objects) are two of the things we find so compelling about beads. And the future is changing.

A beading renaissance began in the late 1980s, and included all types of beading. In addition to beading itself, artisans took up bead making, creating lampwork, blown glass, and polymer clay beads. As beading and bead making gained popularity and markets, the need for gatherings, such as international bead conferences, also expanded.

Soon bead collectors, makers, and artists developed an Internet presence, developing websites, creating blogs, and forming interest groups. Today, a strong sense of being connected around the world can be gained through beads and beading. Picture a string of beads wrapped around the earth many times in every direction, including people in every country, all of them united by their common affection for beads and the art and craft of beading, all of them experiencing a passion that returns them to the very roots of humankind's earliest and most consistent form of adornment. Welcome to the wonderful world of beads!

ALL ABOUT BEADS

The variety of beads available to a beader is astonishing!

Ranging in size from itty-bitty, like a grain of salt, to as big is your fist, beads are created from hundreds of different materials, such as glass, stones, metal, plastic, porcelain, bone, felted wool, and even crushed rose petals. The texture or finish can range from rough to smooth, frosted to glossy, soft to hard, transparent to opaque. Common shapes of beads include round, oval, cubes, tubular, bicone, and disks. Beads are also formed in special shapes such as hearts, flowers, and leaves.

For a reasonable cost, you can quickly acquire quite a stash, stimulating and exciting, calling you to create beaded objects, partly just for the pleasure of doing it. Bead shops are found in most towns and cities; plus there are countless online sources for new and vintage beads. Some resources are listed on page 220.

Glass Beads

Glass is so versatile and is available in so many colors that it has long been a favorite material for making beads. Researchers believe the earliest glass beads were made in Egypt and Mesopotamia and may be dated as early as 3500 BCE.

Today glass beads are classified by the method used to make them. Manufactured worldwide, glass beads are made by huge companies, small businesses, and by artists working in home-based studios.

Lampwork Beads

Lampwork beads (also called flame-worked or wound beads) are made by holding a slender rod of glass in the flame of a torch until the glass at the tip of the rod becomes molten. The lampworker holds a metal rod in the other hand, winding the molten glass around it to create each bead. Beads may be shaped in half-molds or with paddles. When complete, beads are cooled slowly (annealed) to prevent cracks from developing.

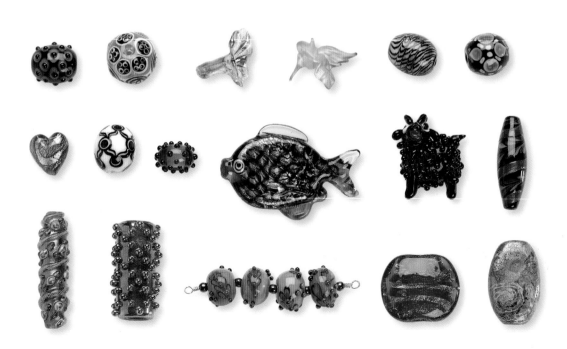

Blown Glass Beads

To create blown glass beads, the maker takes a gather of molten glass from a furnace on the end of a long metal pipe and then blows into the pipe to force air into the glass at the other end, forming a bubble. The glass blower then reheats the glass, attaches a second pipe to the other side of the bubble, and pulls the pipes in opposite directions to create a tube. When the tube is the desired diameter, the glass is cooled, eventually cut into tubular beads, and polished to smooth the cut ends. These types of beads are also called cane glass beads.

Grinding certain areas of the tube produces faceted blown glass beads. Cutting the tubes into thin slices produces disks. Layering different colors of glass over the original gather before pulling the tube yields multi-colored beads. Blowing the molten glass into a mold creates hollow, shaped beads.

Pressed Glass Beads

Pressed glass beads are made by heating a thick rod of glass in a furnace until it is almost molten and then pressing beads with a two-part steel mold that is held in a tong with a retracting pin that makes the hole. Larger beads are pressed one at a time; smaller beads may be pressed in multiples. The beads are annealed, cut apart, ground or tumbled to remove flack around the connection between the two parts of the mold, and then polished. As with seed beads, (page 12), various treatments to the surface of the basic bead extend the range of colors, textures, and finishes available.

Pressed glass beads may be round, oval, bicone, disk, or other standard shapes or special shapes such as hearts, flowers, leaves, drops, or lentils. Pressed glass methods are also used to make faceted beads (not as sharp-edged as crystal beads) and specialty forms such as cats, elephants, and butterflies.

Crystals

Crystal can be a confusing term, because the original meaning of it refers to a naturally occurring rock formation with flat surfaces and defined edges. Transparent glass with lead added to it, used to make fine stemware, glassware, and beads, is also referred to as crystal.

Today, simple shapes of pressed glass beads are ground to create facets (flat, reflective, sharp-edged areas) on the surface of the bead. The resulting beads are called crystals. Swarovski in Austria is the best-known manufacturer of crystal beads, offering them in a variety of shapes, colors, and finishes.

MEASUREMENT OR WEIGHT	SIZE 15	SIZE 11*	SIZE 8	SIZE 6	SIZE 11 DELICAS
Number of beads per inch (2.5 cm) when strung	24	18	13	10	19
Number of beads per gram	260	110	38	15	190
Number of beads per ounce	7,300	3,100	1,075	425	5,350
Number of beads per 6" (15 cm) tube (+/-30 g)	7,800	3,300	1,140	450	5,700
Number of beads per 3" (7.5 cm) tube (+/-15 g)	3,900	1,650	570	225	2,850

Seed Beads

Small, like the plant seeds for which they are named, glass seed beads are manufactured in the Czech Republic, Japan, China, and India. Seed beads are sold packaged loose in containers or stranded in hanks.

Seed beads are available in a variety of sizes. The number designating the size originates from the approximate number of beads it takes to equal 1" (2.5 cm) when they are strung on thread. Many bead shops offer size 15 (small), 11 (most common), and 8 (large). A few shops sell seed beads as small as size 24 (like a grain of sand) or as large as 3 (the size of a pea).

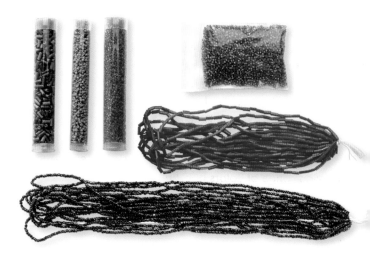

*All seed beads vary greatly in size depending on where they are made, the style of the bead, and the finish on the bead. Size-11 beads, the most commonly available, seem to vary more than other sizes. For example, measured by the length of the hole, Japanese size-11 seed beads can be nearly twice the size of Czech-manufactured size 11s. The quantities specified in the chart above correspond more closely to seed beads made in Japan.

Seed beads come in a remarkable range of colors and finishes. They may be transparent, semi-opaque, or opaque. The color of seed beads is permanent when it's derived from an ingredient in the glass formula. However, to meet the demands of beaders desiring a wider variety of colors, manufactures also make seed beads that are coated on the outside or inside with

paints or glazes. Some of these coatings are relatively stable, whereas others will quickly fade in sunlight or rub off with use.

Color-Fast Test

When making a significant project with seed beads, it is wise to test them for color fastness.

1. Set a few beads of each color in direct sunlight for three days. Check if the color fades by comparing them to originals.

2. Take a nail file or emery board and gently file the surface of a bead. If a surface coating flakes off, this bead will lose its color from friction.

3. Soak a few beads of each color in water to which you've added a little detergent and bleach, and allow to soak for twenty-four hours. Then compare these to the originals.

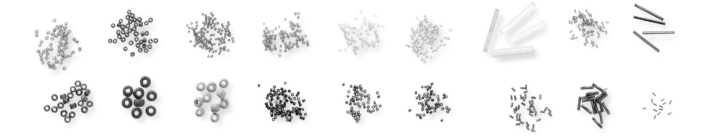

Rounded Seed Beads

By far the most commonly available seed beads have rounded edges and are slightly wider (diameter, measured across the hole) than they are long (measured by the length of the hole). Rounded seed beads are available in sizes 16 through 3 in a wide range of colors and finishes.

Delica Beads

Delica beads are cylindrical in shape and have very thin walls, as opposed to the thicker walls of rounded seed beads, and comparatively large holes. They are generally about the same height as width, making them an excellent choice for many bead weaving projects.

Made in Japan, Delica beads may be identified by the manufacturer's name, such as Toho or Miyuki. They are made in four sizes: 15, 11 (most commonly available), 10, and 8. Size 11 is available in a broad range of colors and finishes, with over 800 to choose from.

Bugle Beads

Bugle beads are longer than they are thick, creating a tubular shape. The diameter of most bugle beads is equivalent to the diameter of a size-12 seed bead. The length may be designated in millimeters (mm) or by a number (#2 is 3/16" [4.8 mm] long; #3 is 1/4" [6 mm] long; #5 is 1/2" [1.3 cm] long). Like other seed beads, bugle beads are available in a variety of lengths, colors, and finishes.

Cut Seed Beads

Sometimes called charlottes, cut seed beads have faceted sides, like miniature crystals. The cut surfaces reflect light, adding a bit of sparkle to beadwork. Cut seed beads are available in sizes 15, 13, and 11 in a wide range of colors and finishes.

Shaped Seed Beads

In recent years, seed bead manufacturers have starting offering shaped seed beads including triangular, cube, drop (with off-center hole), hex, and twisted hex. Shaped seed beads are generally available in sizes 11 and 8, with a few in larger or smaller sizes.

Tip

Many bugle beads are sharp on the ends where the glass tubes have been cut to create designated lengths. Be aware that these sharp edges can cut beading thread, even beading wire. When possible, bracket bugle beads with rounded seed beads to lessen the danger (see page 75). Also, though it takes some time, you can gently file or sand the sharp ends of bugle beads to smooth and round them.

Metal Beads

There is a huge variety of metal beads, some made of precious metals like silver and gold; others of more common metals such as brass, bronze, copper, or pewter; and still others from less expensive or even base metals. Most metal beads are machine made, and so are uniform from bead to bead.

Beautiful sterling-silver beads are handmade in northern Thailand, Bali, and India. Some Native Americans still make sterling beads using traditional metalsmithing techniques. Contemporary metalsmiths around the world cast and fabricate silver and other metal beads.

Tip

Quality sterling silver and gold-filled beads are the most expensive choices. Sterling plated and gold-plated (also called vermeil) metal beads are much less costly, but the plating wears off with frequent use. Gold- and silver-colored metals are the least costly and generally retain their finish well, but don't have a high-quality look.

Stone Beads

Nearly every type of stone can be carved either by hand or by machine, drilled, and polished to make beads of different sizes and shapes. The color of some types of stones can be altered or enhanced by heat-treating or dyeing. Stones may be natural or man made (synthetic).

Glass, Plastic, or Stone?

Say there are three similar-looking beads in a bowl. One is glass, one stone, and one plastic. Can you tell which is which? The plastic bead will feel warm to the touch compared to the other two. If you hold the non-plastic beads, one in each hand, the glass bead will warm up more rapidly than the stone bead.

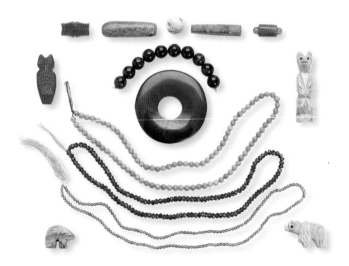

Taking Care of Pearls

Do not store pearls in plastic bags. The bags release chemicals that cause the pearls to lose their luster and sometimes to blister. Store pearls in soft cloth bags or glass jars.

Pearls are sensitive to all types of chemicals. It's best not to wear perfumes on skin that will be touched by pearls. When necessary, clean pearls gently with an unscented, mild soap and allow them to dry completely before putting them away.

Pearls

Whether alone or added to a design made with other types of beads, pearls hold a special attraction for most people. The higher the quality of the pearls, the more lustrous and uniformly shaped they are. Faux pearls are also widely used by beaders.

Natural and Cultured Pearls

Most natural and cultured (induced) pearls are formed either in freshwater mussels or saltwater oysters. They can be perfectly round or irregularly shaped. The outside layer of pearls, called nacre—whether smooth or lumpy, perfectly white, or tinted—has a characteristic lustrous glow. Because nacre is quite porous, it readily accepts dyes without substantially affecting the luminous quality of the surface. Pearls may be dyed to provide a wide range of available colors.

Real or Fake?

Here are two ways to tell the difference between genuine and imitation pearls. When viewed under bright light, real pearls will have slight variations in color and iridescence, whereas faux pearls will all look identical. When you view them under magnification, the characteristic ridges and irregularities of real pearls are distinguishable from the grainy smoothness of imitations.

Imitation Pearls

Very realistic-looking pearls are made from glass beads coated with a pearlescent paint that is baked on the glass to make the finish last. High-quality imitation pearls are available in many bead shops. Plastic pearls are also available.

Polymer Clay Beads

Ever since polymer clay became a popular craft medium in the 1980s, artists have created beads, charms, buttons, and embellishments from it. Polymer clay comes in many colors, which can be blended to create a full spectrum of colors. It can be sculpted into any shape and be formed to imitate more expensive or antique glass, stone, and ivory beads. Once baked (cured), polymer clay beads are durable, holding both their shape and color over time.

Plastic, Resin, and Lucite Beads

Many types of plastics are used to make beads. Lucite beads, made with an acrylic plastic similar to Plexiglas, and beads made from liquid resin in Indonesia are popular because of the available colors and light weight.

Ceramic Beads

Porcelain, stoneware, and earthenware clays of all types can be used to create beads by molding, sculpting, and turning methods. Ceramicists may apply various glazes to the beads, after which the beads are hardened by bringing them to a specific temperature in a kiln.

Bone, Horn, Amber, Coral, and Shell Beads

A wide variety of natural materials may be carved and drilled to create beads. The most commonly available beads of this type are made from bone. The term "heishi beads", originally referring to small, disk-shaped bits of shell that were drilled, now refers to any beads of this shape, including those made from stones.

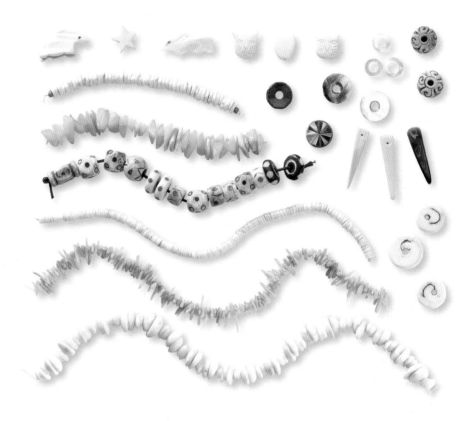

Beads Made from Other Materials

Just about any firm material can be used to create beads. Examples of a few oddities include petals of fragrant flowers such as roses (compressed, formed, and dried), wool or animal fur (felted and pierced), teeth (drilled), paper (rolled and glued), pencil stubs (drilled), and vinyl records (punched and drilled.

Trade Beads

The term "trade beads" refers to beads that are made in one place, and then traded for money, goods or services in a distant location. The term "African trade beads" generally refers to beads made in Europe and traded in Africa between 1800 and 1950 by various trading companies. Also, during the same era, beads made in China were traded in various countries, including the United States. The study and collecting of trade beads is a whole other field within beading.

Trade beads, generally being more than 25 years old and repurposed several times during their journey, carry a patina of mystery and charm that some beaders find irresistible.

Vintage and Antique Beads

Bead collectors may define antique beads as being more than 100 years old, and preferably much older than that. But contemporary beaders are intrigued by any beads that are rare and not currently being made. These are usually called vintage beads. Estate sales can be a good source for vintage beads as well as certain vendors at bead conferences and trade shows.

Charms, Buttons, and Cabochons

Charms with a loop or hole for attaching them are frequently used by beaders as embellishments in their designs. Most charms are metal, including sterling silver, gold, plated metals, bronze, and brass.

Buttons can be used as jewelry clasps and also as decorative elements. Buttons are made from many of the same materials as beads.

Special Objects

Many beaders have a special fondness for domed, flat-bottomed cabochons. Whether carved or plain, a cabochon is often used as a focal point in beadwork. Cabochons are made from many different materials, including stone, glass, bone, and metal.

Hoping to find a way to use them, beaders always seem to collect special objects that aren't beads, buttons, or charms. And this is good, since anything alluring and unique can turn into just the needed pizzazz for a future beading project.

BASIC BEADING KIT

Most beaders have a modest kit of basic tools and supplies always at hand. The exact contents of the kit will vary depending on personal preferences for certain brands and types of beading.

To get started, a beginner can assemble a kit of basic supplies for a very reasonable cost compared to other crafts. For many of the beading techniques and projects included in this book, good lighting, scissors, thread, and needles are all that is needed. However, experienced beaders are likely to have most (or even all) of the following items in their bead kit.

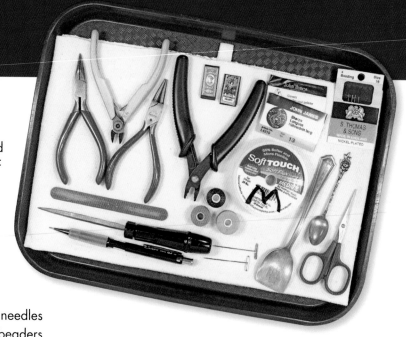

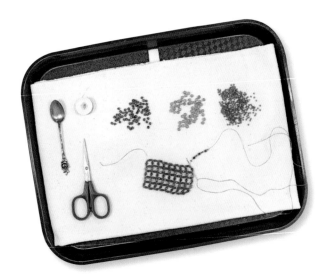

Beading Cloth

A shallow tray lined with an off-white linen napkin makes a good surface on which to lay out piles of beads for a project. It can easily be moved to a different location or covered during beading breaks. Runaway beads are caught by the edge of the tray. Some beaders prefer to line the tray with a thick, acrylic beading mat or a piece of Ultrasuede. When working with white or transparent beads, it helps to have a dark-colored beading cloth.

Scissors and Rulers

Fine, sharp sewing scissors for cutting thread and other fibers is needed for bead weaving, embroidery, and some stringing projects.

For measuring, you will need a standard ruler, marked on one side with inches and the other with millimeters. A tape measure or yardstick (meterstick) is also helpful. Less used, but handy, is a gauge with notched jaws for measuring the diameter of beads, wire, or other objects. It should measure both in inches and millimeters.

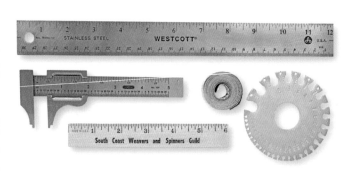

Lighting

Good lighting is very important for working with beads, especially seed beads. To be able to distinguish colors, see the thread path, follow charted designs, and avoid eye strain, use a task lamp with a full-spectrum bulb. Beaders with prescription glasses can ask their optometrist for extra magnification for the working distance between hands and eyes. For those who don't normally wear glasses, quality reading glasses may be useful at times.

Bead Containers

To organize a bead stash, get an adequate number of small containers that are all the same size, for example 2" x 3" (5.1 x 7.6 cm) heavy-duty (4 mil) plastic resealable bags. Transfer beads from their original tubes or bags to the new containers. Group them by color and/or type of bead in larger containers.

Beading Needles

Having a variety of needles on hand will allow you to choose the most appropriate size for a given project. The following sizes are useful: 10, 11, 12, and 13 in both long and short types. Optional: Glover's needles (for beading on leather) in sizes 10 or 11, big eye needles, and twisted-wire needles.

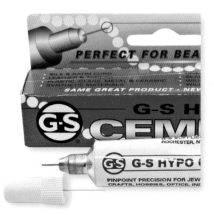

Beading Thread and Wire

For sewing or weaving with beads, use nylon beading thread. Keep a selection of Nymo or Silamide, size D, in black, white, and a variety of others colors on hand. A bobbin of size A or 00 in white is useful when working with very small seed beads or pearls. Fireline, a braided polyethylene thread, average weight of about 10-lb. test, is recommended for some types of bead weaving, especially if the project includes crystals or bugle beads.

For bead stringing, a much larger variety of threads, wires, and cords are appropriate, depending on the project. Staples include the following: Soft Touch stranded beading wire (clear, medium size), Stretch Magic elastic cord (clear, 1 mm diameter), a few feet (meters) of sterling silver-and/or gold-filled wire (size 20 and 18 gauge), and nylon upholstery-weight thread in two or three neutral colors. Certain projects may call for other threads, cords, or wire, which can be acquired as needed.

Thread Conditioner

Microcrystalline wax (also called synthetic beeswax) and Thread Heaven are two thread conditioners that are commonly used, especially for bead weaving. Thread conditioner makes the thread more manageable, prevents tangling, and extends the life of the thread.

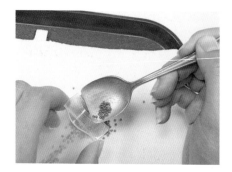

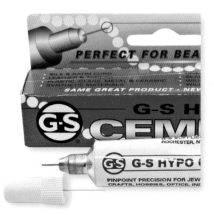

Bead Shovel

To return remaining beads to their containers after beading, use a small spoon or bead shovel. Make an excellent bead shovel by sawing off the tip of a metal spoon, filing the cut edges smooth, and tapping with a hammer to flatten at the cut edge.

Crimping Tool

A quality crimping tool is required for attaching crimp beads at either ends of bracelets or necklaces strung on stranded beading wire. Get one that has two wells in the jaws, one with a little notch in it, and another that is rounded and smooth.

Cement

The most useful cement to have on hand is Hypo-Tube Cement (also called bead-tip or watch-case cement). The fine-tip applicator allows precision gluing of even the smallest knot. White craft glue is also useful.

Wire-Working Tools

It's worthwhile to invest in a few quality tools that can be used for many years. Trying to work with inexpensive pliers and nippers can be frustrating, as their jaws quickly get out of alignment. If possible, take some scrap wire with you while you shop. Try bending and cutting wire with the available tools to see which feel the most comfortable in your hand. Look for pliers with relatively short jaws. The closer your hand is to the working end of the tool, the more control you will have. Test the firmness of the jaw by gently tweaking the handles side to side in opposite directions; less flex signals better quality.

Some pliers and nippers have a spring mechanism that keeps the jaws open until the handles are squeezed. The springs in such tools require effort of the hand to keep them closed in addition to the motion of bending or cutting. Over time, this extra effort is hard on the hand, possibly contributing to medical problems.

Chain-Nose Pliers

Chain-nose pliers have pointed jaws, with a flat surface where the jaws meet. They are used for holding, bending, and twisting wire. They are also useful for pulling a needle through a tight spot, breaking seed beads off a strand, and closing crimp bead covers.

Round-Nose Pliers

Round-nose pliers have round, tapered jaws. They have only one purpose: to make round bends or loops in wire. They are essential for making ear wires, clasps, eye pins, links and for wire wrapping.

Wire Nipper

Wire nippers are used to cut wire. Jewelers use several types of wire nippers. For beaders, a small pair of side-cut nippers is sufficient.

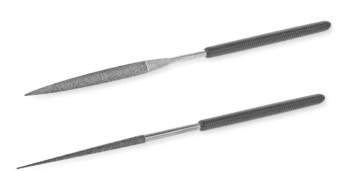

Needle Files

Needle files are small files useful for filing wire, metal components, and bone or wood components. Two shapes are most handy for beaders: barrette and round. Use the barrette file for smoothing the sharp tips of cut wire, to round sharp edges, and to remove dents in wire made by pliers. Use the round file for cleaning, smoothing, or enlarging holes in beads.

Findings

Findings are clasps, ear wires, and other components used in jewelry making. Beaders who are making jewelry tend to accumulate a stash of findings over time.

Findings are available in various metals. The highest quality findings are 14-karat gold, gold-filled, and sterling silver. Using findings made of quality metals gives a professional look to jewelry. The finish on gold- or silver-plated findings tends to wear off quickly, exposing the unattractive, base-metal core.

Less costly bronze, brass, copper, and pewter findings may be appropriate for some jewelry designs. Inexpensive gold- and silver-colored metal findings are also available.

Clasps

There are many types of clasps to choose from, including spring, toggle, pearl, magnetic, hook, box, and multi-strand clasps. Each type is available in various sizes and metals to accommodate the style and weight of your jewelry design.

Make a Clasp

Construct your own S-shaped clasps by bending wire with round-nose pliers.

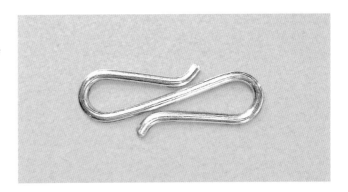

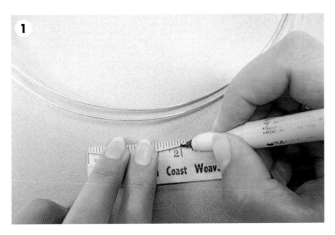

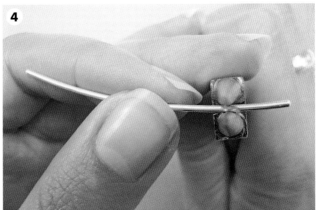

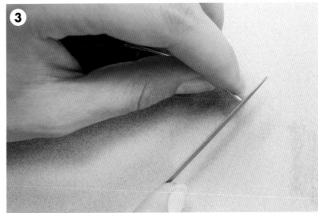

1 Use 20-gauge round wire for small, delicate clasps, 18- or 16-gauge wire for larger, sturdier clasps. Measure 2" (5.1 cm) and mark wire with a felt-tip pen.

2 Use a wire nipper to cut the wire at the mark.

3 Use a flat needle file to file both ends of the wire flat. Then file the ends at an angle to round them slightly.

4 Hold the wire about a fourth of the way from one end with a round-nose pliers at the widest part of the jaws.

(continued)

5 Bend the short end of the wire around the jaw of the pliers until the tip is parallel to the midpoint of the long end of the wire.

6 Repeat step 2 on the other end of the wire, forming an S shape.

7 Lightly grip one end of the wire with the tip of the round-nose pliers and turn it outward. This bent tip will make it easier to catch the clasp in a jump ring. Repeat on the other end.

8 Squeeze the ends with your fingers to close the loops.

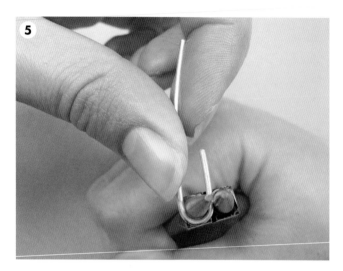

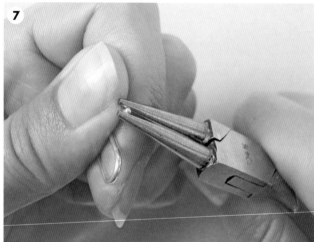

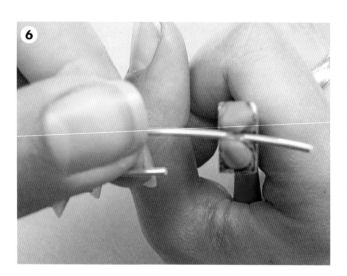

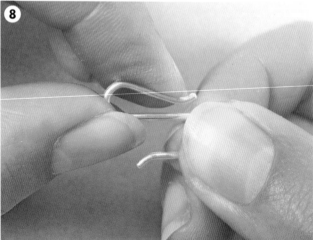

Earring Findings

Ear wires, head pins, and eye pins are the staple findings for making earrings. These findings can be constructed with wire, although often the cost in time and materials is greater than the cost of buying ready-made earring findings.

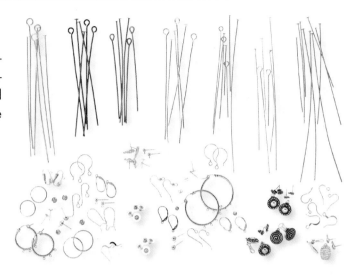

Crimp Beads and Covers

Crimp beads, available in several sizes, are little tubes of metal used to crimp stranded beading wire around clasp attachment rings at the ends of necklaces and bracelets. The most commonly used size is 2 mm long by 2 mm diameter. Select smaller crimp beads for fine-gauge wire and jumbo crimp beads for heavy-gauge wire. Optional: Close a cover over each crimp bead to disguise it, making it look like a round bead.

Jump Rings

Jump rings, circles or ovals made of wire, are used to connect components of jewelry, such as a clasp to a necklace. They may also be linked to each other, forming a chain. Use a soldered jump ring as the matching half of a clasp or hook. Use unsoldered jump rings to connect components. Use split jump rings (like a key ring) when a firm yet unsoldered connector is required.

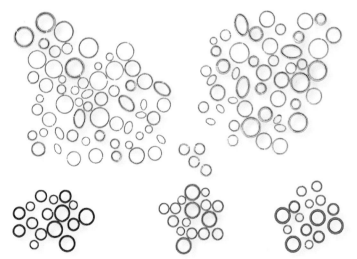

BEAD STRINGING

Bead stringing is the customary entry into beading. The techniques are easy to learn, yet fun and challenging because of the infinite variety of beads available. The process of arranging beads to create pleasing combinations of color and pattern is a good way to learn principles of design. Because bead stringing takes relatively little time and requires minimal expense, strung beads can be worn a few times, cut apart, redesigned, and worn again. Look in bead shops, jewelry departments, and fashion magazines for appealing design ideas.

BEAD-STRINGING TOOLS AND SUPPLIES

You can string beads in lots of different ways, each requiring a few different tools and supplies. For any given design, several stringing methods will work equally well. Beginners generally start with one stringing method, acquiring only the tools and supplies needed for that technique. Later, as they learn about other methods, they begin to build a stringing kit that allows them to select the best method for each project.

In addition to a basic beading kit (see page 20), the following items will prove useful for most methods of stringing beads.

Design Board

A design board, either U-shaped or straight, is useful for laying out the beads in a pleasing design and estimating the finished length of the project. Arrange and rearrange the beads in the groove on the board without concern for the beads rolling out of place or off the table. Some beaders simply use a large, smooth white fabric, such as a tea towel, folded in half or thirds lengthwise as a work surface for spreading out and arranging their beads.

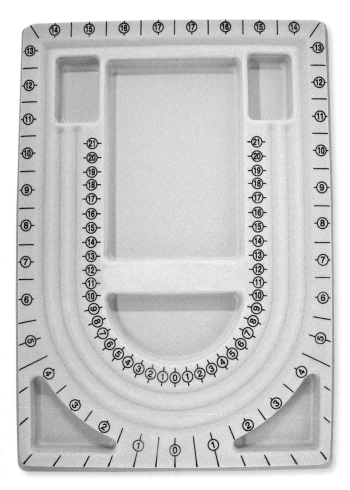

Make Your Own Design Board

If you're handy with wood, make your own design board. Chisel parallel, U-shaped grooves of different widths lengthwise in a 1" x 4" x 36" (2.5 x 10.2 x 91.4 cm) board. Use spray adhesive to attach a thin layer of felt to the board, smoothing it into the grooves. Use a permanent marker to draw a line across the width of the board at the center (18" [45.7 cm] from the end). Make small marks across the top at 1" (2.5 cm) intervals from the center outward. Nail a stopper board on each end.

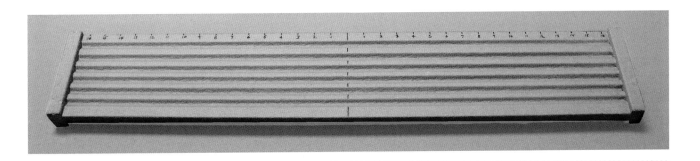

Thread, Cord, and Wire

The techniques and projects in this section are intended to introduce you to several different methods and materials for stringing beads. Stranded wire, elastic cord, and #18 beading cord are the staples of bead stringing. Leather, hemp, linen, artificial sinew, and nylon upholstery thread may be used for some projects. Silk cord, available in many colors and thicknesses, is suitable for hand knotting, especially with quality pearls. Nylon beading threads like Nymo and Silamide, suitable for bead weaving and embroidery, are not strong or thick enough for most stringing projects.

Needles

Some bead-stringing materials do not require the use of needles. Stranded wire, for example, is stiff enough that the end of the wire is used in the same way as a needle. When thread, elastic, or cording is too limp to use as a needle, it's sometimes possible to coat the end with nail polish or Fray Check (a plasticizer, available at fabric shops) to make it stiff enough. If that doesn't work, a needle will be required. Big-eye and twisted-wire needles allow threading larger cords.

If you don't have a needle with a big enough eye, add a harness to a small-eye needle. Thread the needle with about 8" (20.3 cm) of fine beading thread (Nymo, size A or 00). Bring the two thread ends together, tie an overhand knot, and clip the ends ½" (1.3 cm) from the knot.

Thread the stringing material through the resulting harness, or loop.

BASIC TECHNIQUES OF BEAD STRINGING

The projects in the following chapters introduce you to different bead-stringing techniques and finishing methods. The techniques include stringing on elastic, stranded wire, knotted thread, and wire. They are progressive, building in complexity within each chapter.

Selecting the "Right" Stringing Material and Method

When planning a bead-stringing project, keep in mind the value, size, and weight of the beads. Also check the sharpness of the edges of the bead holes and the diameter of the bead holes, and consider the frequency of use. Are you making a bracelet that will be worn day after day, while sleeping and in the shower? Or are you making one that may only be worn for special occasions? Are you making a necklace that needs to look fluid, moving and draping over the body? Or are you making a choker that needs to be a little more rigid? Based on these considerations, choose a stringing method and material that matches the beads and the needs of the piece.

DESIGN AND VARIATIONS

Designing beaded jewelry is both challenging and exciting because of the endless possibilities offered by different types and combinations of beads. Every style can be achieved: contemporary, classic, funky, and everything in between. It's fun to experiment, tweaking the designs in the following projects and those seen in other books, magazines, and shops to fit your own personal taste.

A Few General Principles of Design

Whatever design you choose, it must please you, the designer. Learn to recognize, understand, and please your own aesthetic taste. When you try to please someone else (your family, your friends, or current fashion's concept of beauty) but don't also please yourself, you'll never be totally satisfied with your project.

Your design should be appropriate for its purpose. Consider who will wear your project. If it is a necklace, for example, can the person get it on over her head? Does she have enough dexterity to fasten the clasp? Can she carry its weight on her neck? Will it be appropriate for the type of clothing she wears?

Other critical factors in your design include interest and variety, which may be achieved by providing contrasts in certain variables, such as texture, color, size, value (lightness/darkness), and shape. Too much variety or contrast in too many variables, and your project will look spotty or busy; too little, and it will seem dull. Asymmetry of the bead arrangement will also contribute to the interest and variety of your work.

Unity is also important. When a project possesses unity, the eyes travel around it and don't want to leave it—all the contrasting elements are tied together. Sometimes unity is provided by a theme, concept, or "story" that is told by several elements around the piece. Symmetry and repeating elements will give a sense of unity to your work.

Once the beads are arranged, and before stringing, ask, "What gives this arrangement unity? And what gives it variety? Is there a pleasing balance? How do I feel about it? Is it exciting or a little blah?" Your answers to these questions may lead to a few changes in the arrangement and, ultimately, to a really special design.

Rule of Thumb

Select the strongest and thickest stringing material you can, given the hole size of the beads you wish to string.

STRINGING BEADS
ON ELASTIC

Stringing relatively lightweight beads on stretchy, elastic jewelry cord is a quick, fun way to make a bracelet, anklet, or necklace. Or, using this method, make a set of napkin rings in less than an hour.

Using elastic for jewelry projects offers several benefits, but the main advantage is that the finished piece is easy to put on and take off. Because stringing beads on elastic requires no special tools or findings, it's an appealing way for beginners to experience arranging beads. It's also a useful way to test a jewelry design before stringing

the beads more securely on stranded wire or knotted cord. Stringing on elastic is easy for children, who will enjoy an immediate reward as they slip a completed bracelet over their hand.

One drawback to stringing on elastic cord is that eventually it will lose its ability to stretch. If it breaks or the knot fails, the beads will scatter quickly. For these reasons, it is generally not an appropriate method for stringing rare, valuable beads or beads that have sharp edges, such as crystals and some metal beads.

STAR BRACELET

Stringing Beads on Elastic Cord

Elastic cord is commonly used for making bead bracelets and anklets. Relatively strong and flexible, this stringing material does not require the use of crimps or clasps to close and secure the piece. However, properly tying and gluing the knot in the elastic cord after the beads are strung is important.

As a rule of thumb, select the largest diameter elastic cord that can be strung through the holes of the beads in your design. Although a commonly used size is 0.7 mm in diameter, it's also available in other sizes, such as 0.5 mm and 1 mm, in either clear or black. We use black for this project, as it is easier to see than clear in the photos. However, clear works well for nearly every design.

YOU WILL NEED

- 6" to 9" (15.2 to 22.9 cm) of assorted beads, may include seed beads (see step 1 on page 34)

- one charm, with soldered jump ring (or split ring)

- 14" (35.6 cm) stretch beading cord (Stretch Magic or equivalent), 0.7 mm diameter (see step 2)

- measuring tape or ruler

- jeweler's glue (Hypo-Tube Cement, superglue, or equivalent)

1 Measure the length of a bracelet that fits well. The average or standard length is 7½" (19.1 cm). For larger diameter beads, add an extra ½" (1.3 cm). Lay out the measuring tape on a beading cloth. Arrange the beads and charm along the measuring tape to the desired length. Although beads may be any style or material, avoid beads that have sharp edges at the hole, such as crystals and some metal beads. Select at least one bead that has a hole with a slightly larger diameter. Arrange the beads so the one with the larger hole is the first bead.

2 Test the hole size of the beads on a piece of 0.7 mm elastic cord. If it passes easily through all of the beads, consider using a larger diameter elastic. If it won't pass through certain beads, consider substituting beads with larger holes. If there are no appropriate substitutions, try 0.5 mm elastic cord. If the elastic still doesn't fit through the bead holes, consider a different stringing material and method, such as stranded wire (see page 36).

3 Unwind about 1' (30.5 cm) of elastic cord from the spool. Do not cut it yet. Use the tip of the cord as a needle, and string the bead arrangement from step 1, starting with the bead with the largest hole.

Variations

To make an anklet, increase the cord length and number of beads to fit around the ankle. Generally the measurement will be 10" to 11" (25.4 to 27.9 cm) for a comfortably loose fit. To make a set of napkin rings (see page 32), measure around a folded napkin. Generally the measurement will be about 5½"(14 cm), unless the napkins are extra large or made of heavy fabric.

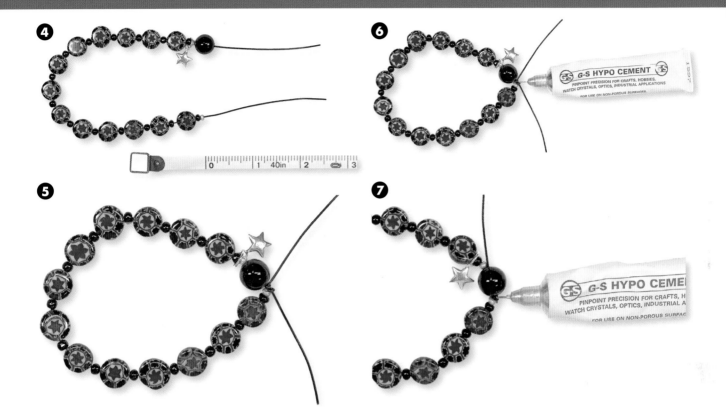

4 Pull the elastic cord through the beads until there is about 3" (7.6 cm) extending beyond the first bead strung. Snug the beads together, and cut the cord from the spool 3" (7.6 cm) beyond the last strung bead.

5 Depending on the diameter of the elastic, tie the two ends together using either a square knot or a surgeon's knot (which is a square knot with an extra twist, also called a double square knot). For 0.5 mm cord, tie a surgeon's knot. For 1-mm cord, tie a square knot. For mid-range cords, try tying a surgeon's knot, but if it seems too large, use a square knot.

To tie a square knot, place the right end of the cord over the left. Bring the right end around and under the left. Pull the two ends tight, stretching the elastic through the beads slightly. Then repeat in the opposite direction, placing the left end of the cord over the right. Wind the left end around and under the right, and pull tight. To tie a surgeon's knot, wind the right end over, around, and under the left twice, making a double twist. Repeat the double twist in the opposite direction.

Do not cut off the cord ends yet.

6 Place a small dab of glue on the knot Allow the glue to dry thoroughly.

7 When the knot is dry to the touch, thread the adjacent cord end through the large-hole bead. Snip the other end of the elastic about 1/8" (3 mm) from the knot. Apply more glue to both sides of the knot. While the glue is still wet, pull on the cord end that exits the large-hole bead and slide the beads around so that the knot is inside the bead with the large hole.

If the cord end will not fit through the large-hole bead, snip both ends about 1/8" (3 mm) from the knot, apply glue, and wiggle the large-hole bead gently to slide it over the knot.

If the knot will not fit inside the large-hole bead, either allow the knot to show or conceal it with a crimp bead cover.

Allow the glue to dry thoroughly before slipping the bracelet over your hand.

STRINGING BEADS ON STRANDED WIRE

Once the beads are arranged, stringing them on flexible stranded wire and attaching a clasp with crimp beads takes only a few minutes. For this reason, it is a widely used method of bead stringing.

Choose a stringing wire that has a fluid feel. Test the wire by unrolling a length and winding it into a fairly tight loop.

Also fold the wire in half and squeeze gently. After you unwind and unfold it, the wire should not have any kinks. Use the heaviest weight of wire possible, given the diameter of the holes of the beads for each project.

Stranded wire jewelry can break due to poor crimping or sharp beads cutting the wire. When that happens, the beads quickly slide off the wire. Thus, for precious or rare beads, such as genuine pearls, it's better to use thread and knot between the beads, as introduced in the next chapter.

TIDE POOL NECKLACE

Stringing Beads on Stranded Wire

This theme necklace is fun to design because you can use many different pressed glass beads, one to six of each type, in all different sizes and shapes. The different shapes provide interest and variety in the design, while the analogous colors and theme-related choices provide unity. To add tactile and visual delight as well, use a few drops and daggers, pointed beads with the hole at one end so they stick out. Select one unifying color of size-8 seed beads to intersperse among the larger beads, particularly next to dagger and drop beads.

The example is 26" (66 cm) long. Adjust the quantity of beads and wire to make a longer or shorter strand. Look for a clasp that complements the theme of your necklace. This type of design will also work with other themes such as spring flowers, fall leaves, babbling brook, and any holiday.

YOU WILL NEED

- 1–2 gram size-8 rounded seed beads

- approximately 100 pressed glass beads in a variety of shapes and sizes

- clasp

- two crimp beads, thick wall, 2 x 2 mm

- 30" (76.2 cm) stranded bead-stringing wire, medium weight

- crimping pliers

1 Arrange the beads along a folded cloth towel or design board. Place larger beads toward the center. Select a unique, larger bead for the center bead and build outward, toward the ends, from there. The beads do not have to be placed in exact order. For each type of bead, place about the same number on each side of the center. They do not have to be the same distance from the center on each side. A little asymmetry works well for this style of necklace.

2 Notice how the arrangement features smaller beads toward the ends and larger beads toward the center. The change is gradual.

3 Cut a 30" (76 cm) length of stranded wire. String a crimp bead on the end of the wire, leaving a short tail of about 1½" (3.8 cm).

(continued)

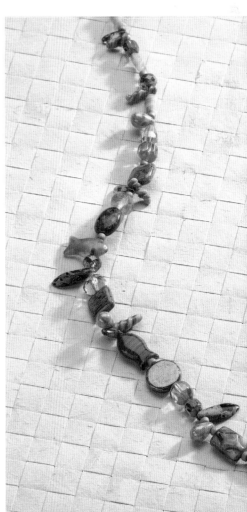

 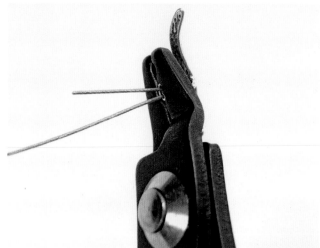

4 String the tail end of the wire through the clasp and then back through the crimp bead. Pull the wire end until the loop is almost snug around the clasp, but still loose enough for the clasp to move freely.

The wire will want to twist, crossing over itself inside the crimp bead. This should be corrected. To make a secure crimp, hold the clasp and the wire so that the wires are parallel, not crossed.

5 Holding the crimp bead in the back notch of the crimping tool, squeeze gently. Examine the crimp. If the spacing looks right and the wires are not crossed, hold the crimp again in the back notch and squeeze firmly.

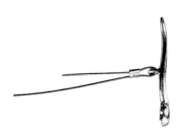  

6 The crimp should look like this. The two wires are each cased now by the crimp bead in a U shape.

7 Turn the crimp bead and wire so that the U-shaped dip faces away from the jaws of the crimping tool and place it in the front notch. Squeeze gently to fold the two sides of the U together. Turn the crimp a few degrees and gently squeeze again. The resulting crimp will look rounded and tubular—like an unused crimp bead only slightly smaller.

8 Select a few beads at the end of the necklace arrangement that have holes large enough to accommodate both wires. String them on the long end of the wire, and push them over the tail end and against the crimp bead. Cover the tail with beads rather than cutting it for a more secure clasp attachment.

- upholstery thread, #69 bonded nylon or equivalent, matching or neutral color

- three beading needles, long, size 10 or 11

- fine nylon thread, Nymo, size A, 0, or 00 (or equivalent)

- glue with toothpick applicator

Size-15 seed beads are only needed if the charms or metal beads have extra-large holes. String a few size-15 beads, and then slide the large-hole element over them. In this way, the large-hole element is supported and centered on the beading thread.

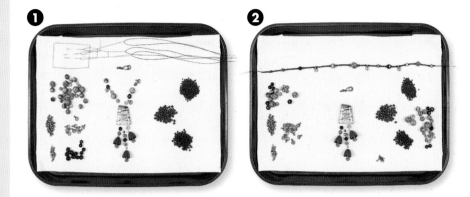

1 Lay out the beads on a beading cloth. Make a tentative arrangement for the tassels. Cut three lengths of upholstery thread, 3 yards (2.7 m) each. Make a harness (see page 30) for each needle. Thread the harnesses with upholstery thread, double it, putting the two ends together. Tie an overhand knot with the ends, leaving a 10" (25.5 cm) tail.

2 Divide the stone beads and metal elements into three groups, one for the tassels and one for each side of the necklace. String size-11 beads, adding larger seed beads, stone, and metal elements spaced about ½" to ¾" (1.3 to 1.9 cm) apart. Use smaller elements at the start of the strand. Gradually increase the size of the elements and frequency of spacing. Knot the strand (see page 41) between two size-11 beads, about every 3" (7.6 cm). Make the strand 12" (30.5 cm) long, or longer or shorter for personal preferences, keeping in mind that the clasp, tassels, and focal bead will add length to the necklace. Knot at the end of the strand. Do not cut the thread or remove the needle.

3 With the second needle, begin a new strand. Lay the new strand beside the completed strand, staggering the placement of the elements in a pleasing way. When the new strand is about 2" (5 cm) long, join the two strands by stitching through one of the larger elements in the first strand. Knot the new strand between size-11 beads approximately every 3" (7 cm).

(continued)

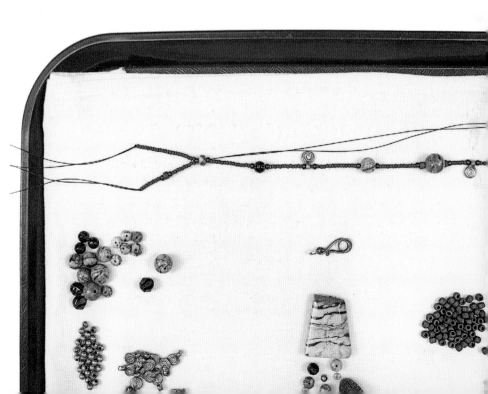

4

5

6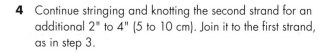

7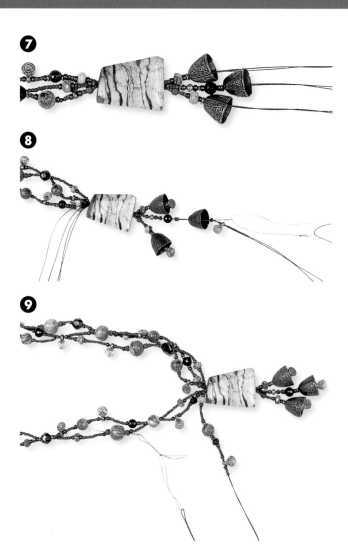

4 Continue stringing and knotting the second strand for an additional 2" to 4" (5 to 10 cm). Join it to the first strand, as in step 3.

5 Continue the second strand, joining it to the first a total of four to six times, until it is the same length as the first strand. Knot the end of the strand.

6 Make a third strand joined at 2" to 4" (5 to 10 cm) intervals to one of the previous strands. Knot the third strand approximately every 3" (7.5 cm) and at the end. One needle at a time, stitch all three strands through the focal bead.

7 String the beads for each of the three tassels, ending with a cone. Adjust the tassel lengths and placement of elements as needed to achieve the desired arrangement.

8 String an ending for each of the tassels, which in this case is a loop of size-15 beads with one of the charms centered. Stitch back up through the beads of the tassel and through the focal bead.

9 Using any one of the needles, string a 12" (30.5 cm) strand for the other half of the necklace. Use larger elements spaced closer together at the focal-bead end of the strand. Tie a knot about every 3" (7.5 cm). Make two more strands, joining them together in the same ways as the other side of the necklace. Knot about every 3" (7.5 cm) and at the end of each strand. Test the necklace for length, adding beads evenly to all strands if it needs to be longer.

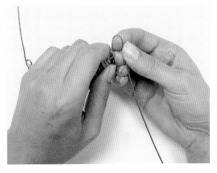

4 Holding the coils, one in each hand, bring the coils toward each other to make a smooth, smile-shaped curve in the wire holding the beads.

5 Loops and Spirals
Hold the pendant as shown, and bend the wire around the tip of your finger, about 1" (2.5 cm) above the coil. End with the wire pointing downward. This makes the first loop.

6 Reposition your fingertip and bend the wire around it, a little below the coil. End with the wire pointing upward. This makes the second loop.

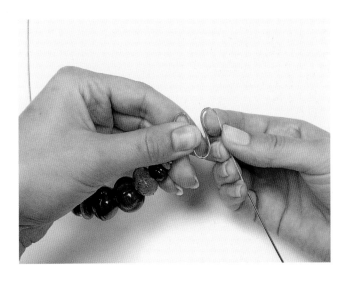

7 Reposition your fingertip and bend the wire, slightly below the first loop. End with the wire pointing downward. This makes the third loop.

8 Measure 4" (10 cm) down from the top of the third loop and make a mark. Cut off the excess wire at this mark. File the cut end of the wire to smooth and round it slightly.

(continued)

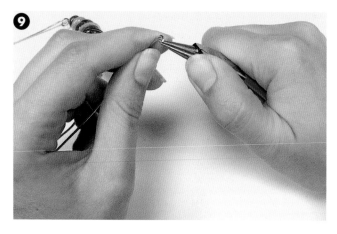

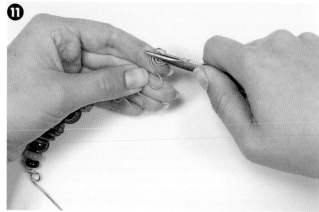

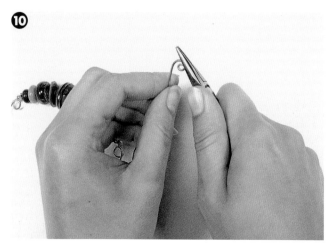

9 Grasp the tip of the filed wire with the tips of the round-nose pliers. Begin turning the spiral, rolling the pliers toward the loops. After making half a turn, remove the pliers and check to be sure the bend is inward, toward the loops, toward the top of the pendant. Continue to turn the spiral until the tip of the wire goes all the way around the nose of the pliers. Remove the pliers. There should be a small circle of wire at the end. This will be rolled up to form the spiral in the next step.

10 Grasp the circle of wire in the jaws of the chain-nose pliers. Use your fingers to continue bending the wire around the circle, forming a loose spiral. Reposition the pliers as necessary to grasp more of the spiral.

11 Continue with this process until the spiral is centered along the loops (see step 16 photo). Repeat steps 5–11 for the other end of the pendant, keeping the loops as similar as possible in size and shape to the ones on the opposite end.

12 Harden Wire by Pounding
Grip the chasing hammer toward the end of the handle, rather than near the head. Letting it swing downward with its own weight, tap the palm of your hand a few times to get the feel of hammering. Keep the hammer head straight up and down, not tilted, to avoid the edge of the hammer face making dents in the wire.

Position the first loop on the rectangular surface of the anvil. Lightly tap the arc of the loop with the domed face of the hammer. Aim for the center of the arc. Do only a few taps at a time; then check to see how it looks. Notice that the wire is beginning to cup a little. Increase the cupping slightly by lifting the pendant away from the anvil about ½" (1 cm). This will be the back of the pendant.

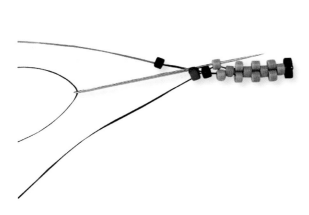

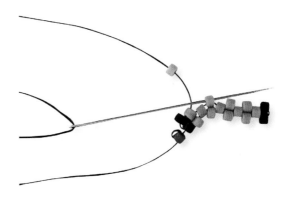

5 To begin the next row, string one black bead. Stitch through bead 15, sewing away from the stop bead.

6 String one lavender bead. Stitch through bead 14, sewing away from the stop bead.

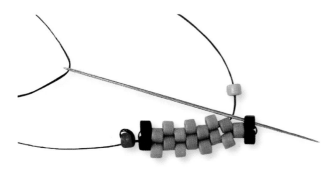

7 Continue to add one bead at a time, skipping every other bead. At the end of this row, string one lavender bead and stitch through the black border bead. Pull gently on the needle and thread to adjust the tension so the beads fit together.

8 The beads now have a brick-like appearance, making it easy to see which beads to sew through and where each added bead fits into the pattern. Continue adding rows working back and forth until there are five black border beads on each end, for a total of ten rows.

(continued)

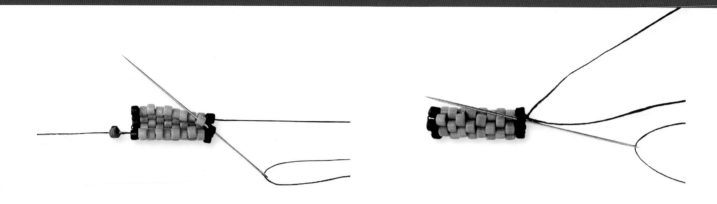

9 Roll the square patch of beads between your fingers to form a tube, with the black beads on each end. Join the sides of the tube by stitching through bead 10 from the first row, then diagonally across to the last bead of row 10, then diagonally across to the next bead in row 1. Continue joining the sides, diagonally from side to side, until the thread exits the black border bead across from the stop bead.

10 Remove the stop bead. Gently pull both threads to adjust the tension so the tube is round and firm. Tie a square knot with the tail and the needle thread. With the needle thread, stitch down through the beads to the other end, making one or two squares along the way. To make a square, stitch down one bead, up the bead next to it, back down the first bead (see page 74). Cut the thread flush with the end of the tube. Thread the tail on the needle and repeat.

11 Make five more woven beads, each in a different main color. Lay out a pattern of spacers, round beads, crystals, and the woven beads to form the desired bracelet length. Following the directions on page 36, string the beads on stranded beading wire, and attach the clasp using crimp beads.

Variations

To make tube beads with transparent or semi-transparent Delicas, match the thread color to the bead color as closely as possible or use a transparent thread, such as Fireline. If these beads have black borders, color the threads at the ends of the beads with a black permanent marker..

To make beads without the black borders, disregard the color directions. For step 1, string eleven beads in one color and continue to work with that color for the remaining steps.

Although tube beads woven from these directions will be about ½" (1 cm) long and ³/₁₆" (4.5 mm) in diameter, they can be made any diameter or length you wish. Always begin with an odd number of beads, weaving until the work rolls into the desired diameter tube and the weaving thread exits opposite the stop bead. To ensure that wider diameter tubes hold their shape, it may help to insert an appropriately sized plastic straw.

STOCKING ORNAMENT

Shaped Flat Peyote Stitch

Decorate a tabletop holiday tree with this cute beaded stocking, stitch it on to cardstock as a greeting card for a friend, or make a whole string of them to festoon a fireplace mantel.

The basic technique is flat peyote stitch, but you will need to increase for the toe and decrease for both the tip of the toe and the heel. Once the methods for increasing and decreasing are learned, you can create any shape with peyote stitch. Although Delica beads are recommended for this project, it could be made with round seed beads. The finished stocking measures 1¾" high by 1⅜" wide (4.4 x 3.5 cm), and takes about two hours to complete.

YOU WILL NEED

- 2 g Delica beads, size 11, white (W)

- 2 g Delica beads, size-11, red (R)

- two pearls, 4 mm, imitation or genuine (for pompoms)

- ½ g round seed beads, size 15 (OK to substitute size-11 or Delicas), red

- beading thread, Nymo or equivalent, size D, white

- beading needle, size 12 or 11

YOU WILL NEED

- 5 g round seed beads, size 11, color A

- 5 g round seed beads, size 11, color B

- 5 g round seed beads, size 11, color C

- beading thread, Nymo or equivalent, size D, neutral color

- beading needle, size 12

- 24" (61 cm) wire, 28 to 30 gauge (for the handle)

- wooden toothpick (or piece of 16-gauge wire)

MINIATURE BASKET

Circular Peyote Stitch and Ruffle

The diameter of this adorable little basket is about 1" (2.5 cm), perfect for holding a ring or two while doing chores. Make one in size-15 seed beads for a dollhouse-size basket.

This basket is worked in rounds of circular peyote stitch, beginning in the center of the bottom. The number of beads in some rounds will be increased to keep the bottom flat while at the same time increasing its diameter. The sides are woven in tubular peyote stitch, which is the same as circular peyote stitch except the number of beads in each round is kept constant. Drastic increasing produces the ruffle at the top. The design uses three colors of beads, which makes it easy to tell which round you are weaving and when to step up to the next round. Complete a basket in about two hours.

Round 1

String six color-A beads on 1½ yards (1.35 m) of beading thread, leaving a 6" (15 cm) tail. Make a circle by stitching through all the beads, starting with the first bead strung. At the end of the circle, stitch through the first bead again. Keep the tension loose for rounds 1–9.

Round 2

Stitch one color-B bead between each bead in round 1. When adding the sixth bead, stitch through the next two beads (the last color-A bead and the first color-B bead). This is called a "step up" to the next round.

Round 3

Stitch two color-C beads between each bead in round 2 for a total of twelve color-C beads in the round. Step up by stitching through two beads (colors B and C). Note that the needle exits between two color-C beads.

(continued)

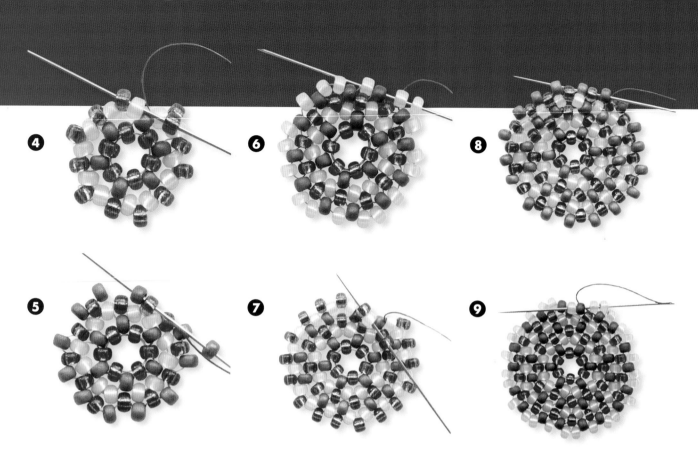

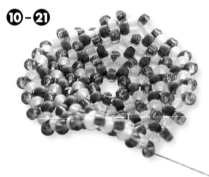

Round 4

Stitch one color-A bead between each bead in round 3 for a total of twelve color-A beads in the round. Step up by stitching through two beads (colors C and A). When adding a bead between sets of two beads, give a slight tug to "click" the middle bead into place.

Round 5

Stitch one color-B bead between each bead in round 4 for a total of twelve color-B beads in the round. Step up by stitching through two beads (colors A and B).

Round 6

Using color C, alternate stitching one bead, then two, then one, then two between each bead in round 5 for a total of eighteen color-C beads in the round. Step up.

Round 7

Stitch one color-A bead between each bead in round 6 for a total of eighteen color-A beads in the round. Step up.

Round 8

Stitch one color-B bead between each bead in round 7 for a total of eighteen color-B beads in the round. Step up.

Round 9

Using color C, alternate stitching one bead, then two, then one, then two between each bead in round 8 for a total of twenty-seven color-C beads in the round. Step up.

Rounds 10–21

The next twelve rounds are worked in tubular peyote stitch, which is the same as circular, except there are no increases. Tighten the tension for these rounds. Alternating the colors (A, B, and C) in the same order as rounds 1–9, stitch one bead between each bead of the previous round. Step up at the end of each round by stitching through two beads. There should be a total of twenty-seven beads in each round. In rounds 11–13 the edges of the circle will become wavy. By round 14, there will be a definite bowl shape. Round 21 will be in color-C beads.

Rounds 22–24

The final three rounds form the ruffle at the top of the basket. For round 22, stitch two color-A beads between each bead in round 21 for a total of fifty-four color-A beads in the round. Step up by stitching through three beads (one color-C and two color-A). For round 23, stitch two color-B beads in each gap; then stitch through the pair of beads in the previous row, keeping the total at fifty-four beads for the round. Step up, passing through three beads as in the previous round. For round 24, repeat round 23 in color-C beads. Bury the tail and any thread ends (see page 74).

Spiral Handle

Stick the wire through two beads in round 20, 21, or 22 (whichever accepts the wire most easily) on the inside of the basket. With the beads in the center of the wire, fold it in half so the two ends are alongside each other. Holding the two wires together, string 6" (15 cm) of beads, alternating colors A, B, and C. Wrap the beaded wires around

a toothpick. Gently pull out the toothpick. Stick the wires through two beads directly across the basket in the same round as the other end. Twist the wires together and snip.

If the wires will not go through the beads in the basket, cut the wire in half, string 6" (15 cm) of beads over both pieces of wire, and with the beads centered on the wires, wind them around a toothpick to make a spiral handle. Poke the wires on one side of the spiral through the basket (just below the ruffle) to the outside. String a few beads on each wire, wind each around a toothpick to make a curl, snip the wires about ¼" (6 mm) from the end bead, and bend the wire back around the end bead to secure the basket handle. Repeat for the other side of the basket.

Variations

In addition to color variations, there are several possible ways to make the handle, including a double wire joined at the top through a single bead or a few flower beads. Leave the top plain, without the ruffle, for a more basic look. Or make the ruffle all one color. Make the basket taller and insert a glass vial to use as a bud vase. Use size-15 seed beads to make a smaller or size-8 for a bigger version of the basket.

BARNACLE BROOCH

Sculptural Peyote Stitch

Once the basics of flat, circular, and tubular peyote stitch are learned, many beaders enjoy the freedom of expression found with sculptural or free-form peyote stitch. For some, it is an intuitive extension that develops easily. For others, a project such as the *Barnacle Brooch* gives needed directions for learning to weave sculptural pieces. Making this brooch will certainly provide enough experience to know if weaving free form is enjoyable for you.

The barnacle, a marine crustacean with an external shell that attaches itself permanently to rocks and other surfaces in the sea, is the inspiration for this sculptural peyote project. Tubular and circular peyote stitches are used to weave a barnacle. The brooch is built by combining a group of barnacles. It is then completed by adding surface embellishments. The finished piece can be worn as a pin or pendant.

YOU WILL NEED

- 5 g seed beads, size 11, any desired main color

- 2 g seed beads, size 15, accent color

- five to ten embellishment beads, stone chips (or equivalent), small

- five beads for barnacle centers, potato pearls (or equivalent), 6–10 mm

- beading thread (6-lb. Fireline recommended, or equivalent)

- beading needle, size 11 or 12

- pin back with attached converter bail (optional, plain pin back)

- mandrel, ½" (1.3 cm) diameter (wooden dowel, plastic tube, pen, or other)

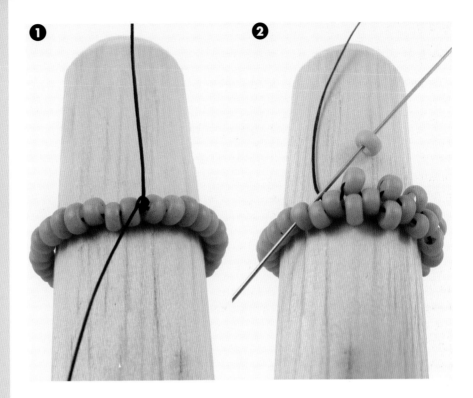

1   Construct a Barnacle
Thread the needle with about 3' (91.5 cm) of beading thread. To form the foundation row of beads for the barnacle, string a sufficient number of size-11 seed beads to circle the mandrel. Use an even number of beads. Secure the circle of beads with a square knot. Leave a 6" to 8" (15 to 20 cm) tail to be woven into the barnacle later.

2   Begin weaving the barnacle using peyote stitch. Stitch through the first bead of the foundation row. String a size-11 bead, and slide the bead down the thread to the foundation row. Skip one bead in the foundation row, and stitch through the next bead in the row. Continue to peyote stitch all the way around the foundation row with size-11 beads.

(continued)

3 Complete the row by stitching through two beads: the last bead in the foundation row and through the adjacent bead in the row just completed. This is called a "step up".

4 Complete two more rows using size-11 beads. At the end of each row, step up to begin the next row.

5 Slip the beadwork off the mandrel and switch to size-15 beads. Hold the ring of beads in your fingers, and add two more rows. Using size-15 beads for these two rows will automatically close the top of the barnacle inward. When the two rows are complete, sew diagonally downward through the beads to position the thread in the foundation row of the barnacle.

6 Begin to weave the base of the barnacle outward using size-11 beads. String two beads and stitch through the nearest up-bead (the one that sticks out) in the foundation row. String one bead and stitch through the next up-bead in the foundation row. Repeat this alternating pattern all the way around the ring thus increasing the diameter for the base. Step up for the next row.

7 For the next row on the base, add one bead per stitch. Be sure to add one bead between each pair of beads used to increase the diameter of the base in the previous row. The first barnacle is now complete.

8 Add More Barnacles
The brooch shape is built by adding a barnacle to the first one, and then another to that group. To begin the next barnacle, string nineteen beads (size-11). Attach this string of beads to the barnacle by sewing through the bead in the last row, which is three up-beads away from where the thread exits the base of the barnacle. This forms the foundation row of the new barnacle.

9 Following steps 2–7, weave the second barnacle. Note that the first two beads added will be part of the base of the first barnacle.

Continue adding barnacles until the shape is pleasing and the brooch is the desired size. The barnacles can be made any diameter (by varying the number of beads in the foundation row) or any height (by varying the number of rows).

Sometimes it's necessary to add another row of peyote

stitch around the base rows of finished barnacles in order to build the desired shape or to position the needle for adding a new barnacle. Also, sometimes you'll need to attach the foundation row of a new barnacle to two of the already woven barnacles in order to form a cohesive shape.

When the barnacles are complete, check the outside border of the brooch to see if another row or rows, or partial rows, of peyote stitch would add a pleasing touch to the overall shape.

(continued)

10 Filling the Barnacles

Filling the barnacles is optional. In this example, potato pearls are used to fill the barnacles. Beads of other materials, such as glass or stone, may be substituted for the pearls. See the variations opposite.

To fill the barnacle, place the bead in the barnacle "shell" from the underside, positioning it as desired. Stitch through the base and barnacle beads to position the needle correctly, and stitch through the filler bead to the other side of the barnacle. Stitch through a seed bead on the other side and then back through the filler bead. Repeat one more time if possible to firmly secure the filler bead. If needed, add another row or rows of seed beads (size 15) at the top of the barnacle to further close it over the filler bead. Select extra-thin beads for this. When the filler bead rests nicely in the barnacle, stitch through beads in the barnacle and base to position the thread for the next filler bead.

11 Adding Embellishments

Attach semiprecious stone chips and/or other assorted small beads randomly to the surface around and between the barnacles. Sew through beads in the base to position the needle for adding an embellishment bead. String the embellishment bead and a seed bead, and then go back through the embellishment bead to the base of the brooch. Repeat.

Note that the above attachment method works well for stone chips and disk-shaped beads. But for some embellishments (such as small drop beads), it's not necessary to add a seed bead and stitch again through the embellishment bead. They can be sewn in place with only one stitch through the hole.

12 Attaching the Pin Back

Sew a pin back to the underside of the brooch. Check the placement of the pin back to make sure the brooch will hang properly. Stitch through beads in the brooch to position the thread to exit under one of the holes in the pin back, and stitch to the surface through that hole. String enough size-15 seed beads to extend to the edge of the pin back, and stitch through a bead in the brooch. Repeat this sequence twice for each hole in the pin back. Bury this thread and any other remaining tails.

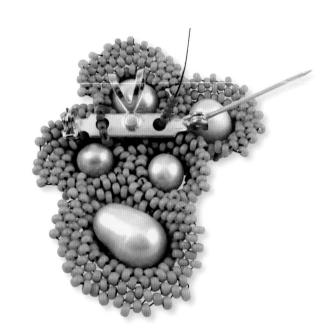

Variations

To create barnacles with an organic look, experiment with using multiple colors and finishes of seed beads. Add further visual interest and texture by using a few triangle seed beads (size 11) in the borders of the barnacles.

RIGHT-ANGLE WEAVE

Right-angle weave, often abbreviated as RAW, is characterized by small, interconnected squares of beads. When done with a single bead for each side of the square, the resulting woven piece is like fabric, dense and fluid. In fact, historical examples of this technique include clothing made entirely of woven beads in this stitch. There are several variations in the way the stitch is done. Some older versions, like those practiced in Russia a century ago, use two needles.

The project in this chapter is a contemporary version, woven with one needle. Although it may take a few tries to completely understand the thread path and be able to weave without referring to the instructions, once mastered, right-angle weave has many possibilities for both jewelry and three-dimensional objects.

AUTUMN CRYSTALS BELT

Right-Angle Weave

Depending on the beads used to make this belt, it can look casual to classy. The belt looks great whether it's worn with jeans, tunics, skirts, or dress slacks. Once the method of right-angle weave is mastered, it will take four to six hours to complete a belt.

In right-angle weave, it is important to understand that the stitch is made up of connecting squares. The sides of the squares can each have one bead or several beads. After making the first full square, each added square will then utilize the sides of the adjacent square or squares plus two or three new sides to complete a new square. In this pattern, each side consists of three beads. The sides are noted as N, S, E, and W. In the pictures, the tail is always exiting the NW (top left) corner.

To master right-angle weave and learn the thread path, it is important to follow both the pictures and the written instructions at first. After a few rows, the weaving process will become intuitive—easy to do without referring to the instructions.

YOU WILL NEED

• 21 g seed beads, size 11, color A

• 840 beads, 3 mm, faceted, color B

• 14 g seed beads, size 6, color C

• 2 g seed beads, size 15, color D

• one three-strand, magnetic, tubular bar-clasp (or similar)

• beading thread (Nymo D, 6-lb Fireline or equivalent)

• beading needle, size 11

The quantities listed are for a 27" (68.6 cm) belt. Adjust the amounts up or down to change the length.

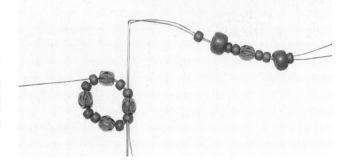

1 String twelve beads: A B A, A B A, A B A, A B A. Slide the beads down the thread and leave an 8" (20 cm) tail. Make a square with the beads by bringing the needle up through the bottom (closest to the tail) and through all the beads in the string. Stitch around the first square clockwise through the next A B A, A B A. The tail exits the NW (top left) corner and the needle end of the thread exits at the SE (lower right) corner.

In the following pictures, the orientation of the beadwork never changes. N is always at the top and W is always to the left.

2 String nine beads: A C A, A B A, A C A. Stitch down through the E side of square 1 and pull tight. This forms the second square.

(continued)

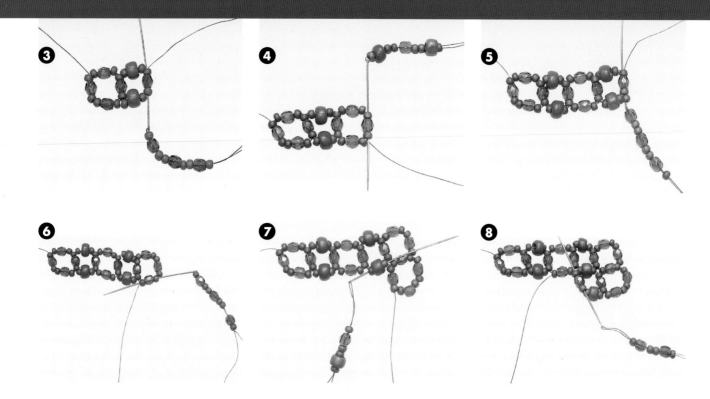

3 Stitch counterclockwise around the S and E sides of square 2. Exit at the NE corner of square 2.

String nine beads: A B A, A B A, A B A. Stitch up through the E side of square 2 and pull tight. This forms the third square.

4 Stitch clockwise around the N and E sides of square 3. Exit at the SE corner of square 3.

String nine beads: A C A, A B A, A C A. Stitch down through the E side of square 3 and pull tight. This forms the fourth square.

5 Stitch counterclockwise around the S and E sides of square 4. Exit at the NE corner of square 4.

String nine beads: A B A, A B A, A B A. Stitch up through the E side of square 4 and pull tight. This forms the fifth and last square of row 1 of the design.

6 Stitch clockwise around the N, E, and S sides of square 5. Exit at the SW corner of square 5.

String nine beads: A B A, A B A, A B A. Stitch through the S side of square 5 in the previous row and pull tight. This forms square 6, the first square in the row 2.

7 Stitch clockwise down the W side of square 6. Exit at the SW corner of square 6.

String 6 beads: A C A, A B A. Stitch through the S side of square 4 in the row above and pull tight. This forms square 7, the second square in the row 2.

8 Stitch clockwise through the E, S, and W sides of square 7 and counterclockwise through the S side of square 3 in the row above. Exit at the SW corner of square 3 in the row above.

String six beads: A B A, A B A. Stitch up the W side of square 7 and pull tight. This forms square 8, the third square in the row 2.

Variation

To create a beautiful bracelet, stop beading when the weaving is about 7" (18 cm) long, and add the clasp.

9 Stitch counterclockwise through the N and W sides of square 8.

String six beads: A C A, A B A. Stitch through the S side of square 2 in the row above and pull tight. This forms square 9, the fourth square in row 2.

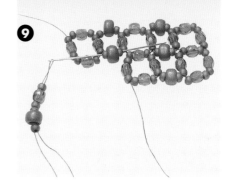

10 Stitch clockwise around the E, S, and W sides of square 9 and counterclockwise through the S side of square 1 in the row above.

String six beads A B A, A B A. Stitch through the W side of square 9 and pull tight. This forms square 10, the last square in row 2.

Important: Before beginning row 3, look closely at all the intersections between the squares. You should see how the thread creates a little hole at each intersection and does not cross through it diagonally. If the thread goes around the intersections, you have successfully completed two rows of RAW bead weaving. If the thread crosses any of the intersections, you may want to cut the weaving apart and try again.

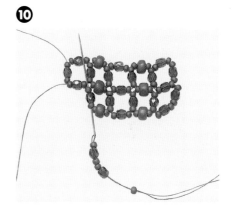

11 To prepare for the first square of row 3, stitch counterclockwise through the N, W, and S sides of square 10. String A B A, A B A, A B A. Stitch through S of square 10. This forms square 11. To continue row 3, repeat steps 7–10, stitching in the opposite direction. Always position the thread for a new square so that it can be made without a vertical or horizontal thread path through the corner.

Continue making rows of five squares each, until the belt is the desired length. All even rows will be the same as row 2 (steps 6–10); all odd rows will be the same as row 2, but stitched in the opposite direction.

When the belt is the desired length, add one side of the clasp to the end. Center the clasp. Stitch through the last row of beads, catching the clasp loops as you go. Stitch around a square and back to the last row of beads. Stitch along the row again, catching the clasp loops as you go. Repeat as many times as possible.

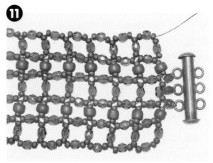

12 To strengthen the belt and square up the weaving, stitch back through all the weaving, filling the small hole at the intersections between each of the squares with a size-15 bead. Position the needle at the corner of the last row of beads. Add a size-15 seed bead and stitch through the next three beads. Add another size-15 seed bead and stitch through the next three beads. Continue this step up and down each row to the other end of the belt.

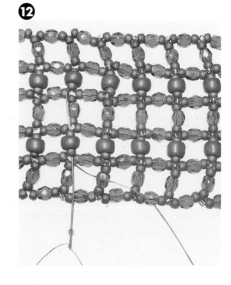

Attach the other half of clasp on the opposite end of the belt. If the clasp you chose will only close when oriented one way, put the clasp together when stitching it to the second end. This will ensure you have both sides of the clasp positioned in the right direction.

BRICK STITCH

Brick stitch, named because it looks like a brick wall when worked flat, is also called Comanche stitch because it has been widely used by the Comanche tribe of Native Americans for two centuries. The earliest examples—from before glass seed beads were available—are made with shell wampum. The Cheyenne and Iroquois tribes also use this stitch now and historically. Some older bead weaving done in brick stitch, dating back to the 1700s, comes from Guatemala, Africa, and the Middle East.

Turned on its side, a piece of brick-stitch weaving will look exactly like a piece of peyote stitch weaving. The only way to tell the difference is to pull the work apart enough to determine the thread path. Both stitches provide the beader with the flexibility to create shaped and dimensional objects. Beaders tend to develop a preference for one or the other.

The characteristic technique of brick stitch involves looping over the thread going between beads in the previous row to attach each bead or group of beads in the new row. By completing the *Vermillion Heart Pin* project, you will learn the fundamental methods of flat brick stitch, along with increasing and decreasing methods to create a shaped piece. The Fan Earrings project (page 104) introduces techniques of circular brick stitch.

YOU WILL NEED

- 2 g seed beads, size 11
- 2 yards (1.8 m) beading thread, Nymo or equivalent, size D
- one pin back, ¾" (1.9 cm)
- beading needle, size 11 or 12

VERMILLION HEART PIN

Shaped Brick Stitch

This sweet little heart pin takes only an hour or so to make. Brick stitch is an intuitive technique, one that is well suited to designing variations, especially for color combinations. After completing one pin in a solid color, creating variations will be easier than you might think.

1 String eight beads on 2 yards (1.8 m) of thread, and slip the beads to the approximate center of the thread.

2 Stitch back through the first four beads (toward the center), and align the second four beads beside the first four beads. Then stitch through the remaining four beads to make two columns. Both threads exit from the same side of the column.

(continued)

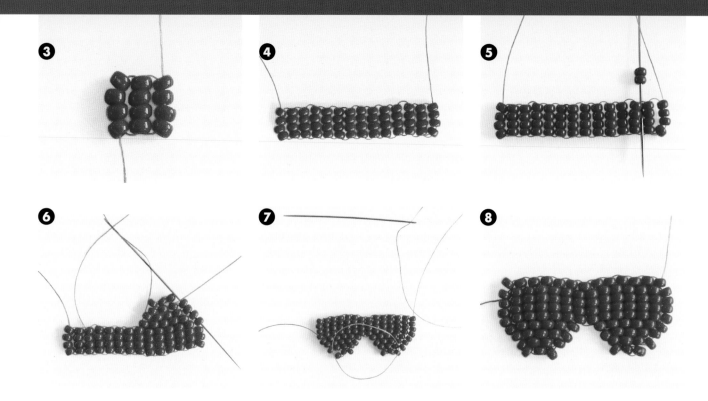

3 String four beads and stitch through the previous four beads and then the four beads just added. Now there are three columns.

4 Continue adding four-bead columns until there are fourteen columns.

5 Flip the work, string two beads and stitch under the thread joining the second and third columns. Then stitch up through the second bead added from the underside where it touches the column.

String one bead and stitch under the next visible thread joining the columns of beads. Then stitch up through the new bead. This is a brick stitch. Each bead in the new row

is anchored to the previous row by stitching under a thread between two beads in the previous row and then up through the newly added bead. Continue in brick stitch until six beads have been added.

6 Flip the work. As in the previous step, start the row by stringing two beads. Continue the row, adding one bead at a time for a total of five beads. Repeat this process, adding one bead fewer for each row until the top is only three beads wide. This is the final row of one of the humps at the top of the heart. At the end of this row, rather than stitching back up through the last bead, stitch down through the edge beads and exit at the base of the column.

7 For the second hump, rethread the needle with the other end of the thread. Repeat steps 5–6 to complete the second hump. Like the other hump, rather than stitching up through the last bead added, stitch down through the edge beads, exiting at the base of the column.

8 Turn the heart upside down. It should look like the picture above. Work the point in the same manner as the humps. Begin each row with two beads; stitch under the thread between the second and third beads below and up through the second bead added. Then add one bead and anchor it with a brick stitch. Continue adding beads across the row for a total of thirteen beads. Each successive row will have one fewer bead. Continue until you reach the two-bead row.

9 When adding the last bead of the two-bead row, rather than stitching up through the last bead added, stitch through the outside edge of the beads, exiting at the base of the column, as shown right. Stitch up and down through adjacent beads, positioning the thread so it exits somewhere in the middle of the heart. Rethread the needle with the other thread and stitch through the outside edge of the beads, exiting at the point. Then stitch through beads, positioning the thread so that it exits next to the other end of the thread. Tie a square knot and bury one tail by stitching up and down through about eight beads.

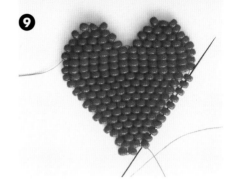

10 Rethread the needle on the other tail and stitch through beads as needed to position the thread for attaching the pin back. Stitch up through one of the holes of the pin back. Crossing to the outside edge of the pin back, stitch through the heart to the front. Stitch through the closest bead toward the hole. Then stitch to the back through the hole. Repeat two or three times on each side of the hole. Stitch up and down through adjacent beads to position the thread at the next hole and repeat. After the pin back is firmly attached, make several half-hitches, and bury the tail by stitching up and down through about eight beads.

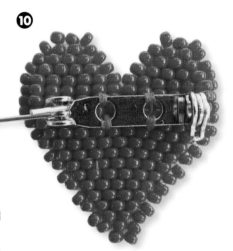

Variations

Make a grayscale scan or copy of a completed pin, enlarged to about 300 percent. Use colored pencils or markers to chart a multicolor design, such as the two shown below.

Use size-15 seed beads to add a picot edge (page 177) around the entire heart, as shown in the third example below.

To make a larger heart, begin with more center columns and readjust the width of the humps accordingly. A larger heart may need some support on the back. Cut the shape out of rigid plastic, and stitch the pin back to the plastic. Cut the shape out of nonwoven fabric, cut holes for the pin back, and place it over the pin back. With the plastic sandwiched between the beaded heart and the fabric, whip stitch around the edges or join them using a picot-edge stitch.

FAN EARRINGS

Circular Brick Stitch

These fan-shaped earrings are fun to wear and can be made in many different color combinations to suit any occasion. Use bright colors for a casual look, metallic beads for a dressier look.

The technique—circular brick stitch—is intuitive and easy to learn. The second earring will only take about one hour to complete. The basic design and color pattern can be modified to create many unique variations.

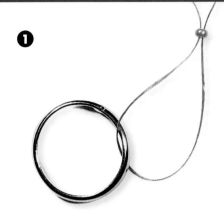

1 Prestretch the beading thread. Cut a piece 3½' (1 m) long and thread the needle. String one color-A bead (size 15), leaving an 8" (20 cm) tail. With the bead and tail on the outside of the ring, stitch through the ring and then back through the bead so the working thread and the tail both exit the top of the bead. Pull the bead tight against the ring, keeping it on the outside edge.

2 String another color-A bead. Stitch through the ring and back through the same bead from the underside. Pull the thread tight. Make sure the second bead sits right next to the first on the outer edge of the ring and the thread exits outward.

3 Continue adding color-A beads one at a time in the same way until the beads extend all the way around the ring. It is better to end with a small gap, using the tread tension to tighten the space, than to force an extra bead into an area too small for it to fit. The beadwork needs to lie flat. Forcing too many beads into a round will cause the work to ripple.

4 To close round 1, insert the needle in the top hole of the first bead of the round. Stitch through the bead and pull the thread to even out the bead spacing and close any gap between the first and last bead of the round.

(continued)

(continued)

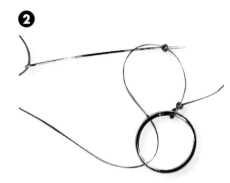

YOU WILL NEED

- 5 g seed beads, size 15, color A
- 5 g seed beads, size 11, color B
- 5 g seed beads, size 11, color C
- beading thread, Nymo or equivalent, size B
- beading needle, size 12
- two metal rings, 12 mm diameter, 18–20 gauge round or half-round wire, must be soldered closed
- two earring hooks

Supply Notes

Because the hole sizes in different beads vary slightly, a size-15 beading needle might come in handy. A size-12 needle will work with most beads. The quantities listed for beads are approximate, but should be sufficient to make at least two earrings. Select beads that are uniform in size, both in diameter and hole height.

5 Stitch up through the second bead in round 1 from the underside of the bead, exiting outward. Tighten the tension to even out the beads around the ring. Ignore the tail. It will be used later, when the earring is complete, to smooth the edge of the fan. Round 1 is complete.

6 Begin round 2 by stringing two color-A beads.

7 Working in the same direction (counterclockwise) around the ring, stitch under the thread between beads 3 and 4 of the first round.

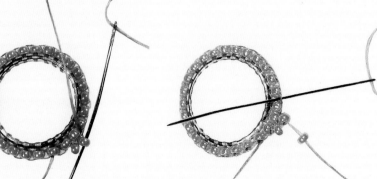

8 Stitch up through the second bead in round 2 and pull the thread snug. The first bead of round 2 will tip slightly. This will be corrected at the end of the round.

9 String another color-A bead. Stitch under the thread between beads 4 and 5 in round 1. Stitch back up through the bead just added to anchor it in place. This is brick stitch.

Continue working in brick stitch all the way around the ring, anchoring at least one bead to the thread between each of the beads in round 1. Because round 2 is larger in diameter than round 1, it will take more beads to go around the circle. Increase four times on round 2 at even intervals.

To increase, add two beads (one at a time), stitching twice under the thread going between two beads in the previous round.

Complete round 2 by stitching down through the first bead and back up from the underside of the second bead of round 2, as in steps 4 and 5. Pull the thread snug and use your fingers to even out the bead spacing in the round.

YOU WILL NEED

- 5 g seed beads, size 11, color A

- 3 g seed beads, size 11, color B

- 6 g seed beads, size 11, color C

- 3 g seed beads, size 6, core color

- one clasp or button

- beading thread, Nymo D, 6 lb. Fireline, or equivalent

- beading needle, size 10 or 11

SUMMER BREEZE BRACELET

Netted Oglala Butterfly Stitch

This netting technique is derived from the Oglala butterfly stitch, created by the Lakota Sioux. In this variation there are two layers of ruffles in hot, vibrant colors to set the mood for a tropical summer day. For an evening look, consider making this project in black, silver, and gray metallic beads. You can also substitute a metal clasp for the button and loop closure, attaching it in the same way.

Although it looks fancy and complex, it's easy to learn how to make this bracelet and it takes less than two hours from start to finish. This bracelet is a good choice for a first netting project.

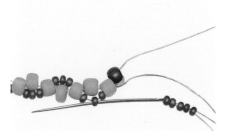

1 String and secure a stop bead on 2 yards (1.9 m) of beading thread, leaving a 10" (25.5 cm) tail. String an even number of core beads to a length of about 7" (18 cm) or (1" to 1½" [2.5 to 3.8 cm] less than the desired length of finished bracelet).

String three A beads. Skip the first core bead and stitch through the second. String three A beads, skip the third core bead, and stitch through the fourth. Repeat, adding three A beads to every other core bead for the length of the core. Do not stitch through the stop bead. Row 1 is complete.

2 String five A beads. Stitch through the second bead of the first A group of row 1. String five A beads. Stitch through the second bead of the second A group of row 1. Repeat this pattern for the length of the bracelet. Row 2 is complete. The stop bead in this example is a dark green color.

3 Periodically tighten the core beads by holding the tail in one hand while pressing the core beads toward the other end of the bracelet with the other hand.

String two A, three B, and two A beads. Stitch through the third bead in row 2. String two A, three B, and two A. Stitch through the third bead of the next group of five beads in row 2. Repeat this pattern for the length of the bracelet. Row 3 is complete

(continued)

4 String three B, three C, and three B. Stitch through the second B bead in row 3. String three B, three C, and three B. Stitch through the second B bead in the next group in row 3. Repeat this pattern for the length of the bracelet. Row 4 is complete.

5 String thirteen C beads. Stitch through the second C bead in row 4. String thirteen C. Stitch through the second C bead in the next group in row 4. Repeat this pattern for the length of the bracelet. Ruffle 1 is complete.

6 Stitch up through the end beads of the ruffle to position the needle between the first core bead and the stop bead.

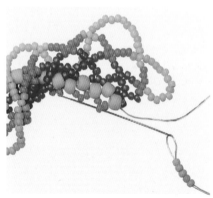

7 Begin ruffle 2. String three B beads. Skip the first core bead and stitch through the second. String three B beads. Skip the third core bead and stitch through the fourth. Repeat, adding three B beads to every other core bead for the length of the core. Row 1 of ruffle 2 is complete.

8 String five C beads. Stitch through the second bead in row 1, ruffle 2. String five C beads. Stitch through the second bead of the next group in row 1, ruffle 2. Repeat this pattern for the length of the bracelet. Row 2 of ruffle 2 is complete.

9 String seven A beads. Stitch through the third bead in row 2, ruffle 2. String seven A beads. Stitch through the third bead of the next group in row 2, ruffle 2. Repeat this pattern for the length of the bracelet. Ruffle 2 is complete.

10 Stitch up through the end beads of the ruffle to position the needle exiting from the last core bead. String a sufficient number of A, B, or C beads to make a closure loop for the button. Stitch back through the first three strung beads.

Stitch through a few core beads and then through some of the beads in ruffle 1. Tie a half-hitch knot. Test that the loop is large enough to

slide easily over the button. Stitch through the beads to position the needle so it exits the last core bead. Tie several half-hitch knots along the path. Stitch through the beads of the loop again. Repeat several times, taking a different path and making a couple half-hitch knots each time. When it's not possible to stitch through the loop another time, stitch into one of the ruffles, and snip the thread.

11 Remove the stop bead. Thread the tail on the needle. String five beads more than half the diameter of the button. String the button. String the same number of beads, less three. Stitch back through the first three beads strung, a few of the core beads, and then through some of the beads in ruffle 1. As in step 10, stitch through the button attachment as many times as possible, stitching into different parts of the ruffles and making half-hitches along the path. Stitch into one of the ruffles and snip the thread.

Variations

To make a matching necklace with three ruffles, first string core beads for the appropriate length. Follow steps 2–5 for ruffle 1. Begin the second ruffle 3" (7.5 cm) from the end of the core and stop 3" (7.5 cm) from the other end. Follow steps 7–9 for the second ruffle. Begin a third ruffle 5" (10 cm) from the end of the core and stop 5" (10 cm) from the other end. The third ruffle is a repeat of ruffle 1, steps 2–5.

LATTICE COLLAR

Netting Worked Up and Down

The village women of Transylvania, in northwest Romania, have created and worn many types of beaded adornments for more than 200 years. The *Lattice Collar* is one example of the beadwork from this area.

Worked up and down in columns, rather than in rows, the pattern is repeated until the strip of netting is about 26" (66 cm) long, at which point the two ends are woven together. The collar slips over the head, draping beautifully on the chest. It can have a very elegant or more casual look, depending on your choice of beads. Relatively easy to learn, the *Lattice Collar* takes less than a day to make.

YOU WILL NEED

- 10 g of seed beads, size 11 or 10, color A

- 45 g bugle beads, 3 or 6 mm, color B

- beading needle, size 10 or 11

- beading thread, Nymo D, Fireline, or equivalent

- jeweler's glue

  It is important to select bugle beads that are uniform, both in length and diameter. Avoid choosing bugle beads that have noticeably sharp or jagged edges.

1   Working with about 5' (1.5 m) of thread, secure a stop bead, leaving an 8" (20.3 cm) tail. String five beads: ABABA.

2   Stitch through the first A bead toward the tail, forming a triangle. This triangle, at the top of the woven strip, will be at the neck edge of the necklace.

(continued)

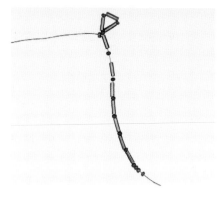

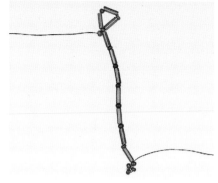

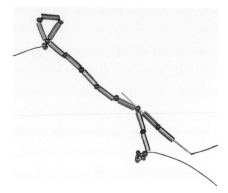

3 String seventeen beads: BA BA BA BA BA BA BAAAA. The last four seed beads will be formed into a diamond. This diamond, at the bottom of the woven strip, will be at the outside edge of the necklace.

4 To begin the upward weave, stitch up through the fourth seed bead from the bottom. Pull upward on the thread to shape the beads into a diamond.

5 String three beads: BAB. Skip two bugle beads and stitch up through the next seed bead.

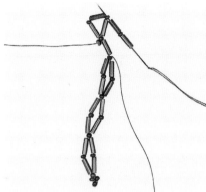

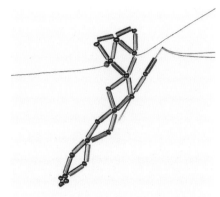

6 Repeat step 5 three times. The last BAB combination of the column attaches to the seed bead at the top of the triangle that was formed in step 2. This completes the upward weave.

7 Begin the downward weave by stringing three beads: BAB. Stitch downward through the first seed bead, forming a second triangle at the top. Tighten the thread a little to make sure all the beads are touching each other with no loose thread between them.

8 String three beads: BAB. Skip two bugle beads and stitch down through the next seed bead.

Adding New Thread

When the weaving thread is 6" to 8" (15 to 20 cm) long, stop weaving at the top of the strip, just below the triangle, and tie on a new thread using a double square knot. After the necklace is finished, apply glue to the knots and then bury the tails by stitching through the beads to the outside edge of the necklace.

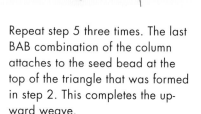

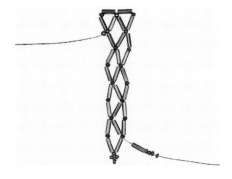

9 Repeat step 8 two times. Then string five beads: BAAAA. This completes the downward weave.

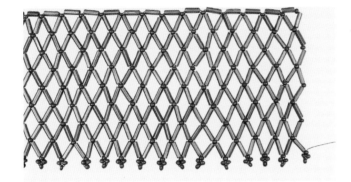

10 Continue to stitch up (steps 4–6) and down (steps 7–9). At the top and bottom of each weave, check the tension, pulling any loose thread snug between the beads. However, since the collar should drape in a fluid manner, don't pull the thread so tight that the weaving becomes stiff.

Weave until the strip measures the desired length. It must be long enough to fit easily over your head, as it is a continuous collar-type necklace with no clasp. For most people, 26" (66 cm) is a comfortable length. End the strip with a diamond at the bottom.

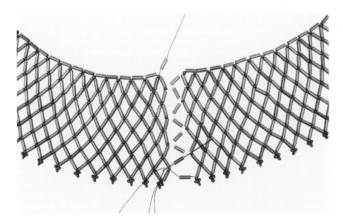

11 Form a circle with the strip, bringing the end around to meet the beginning. Be sure there are no twists in the strip. Stringing one bugle bead for each stitch, lace the end to the beginning, weaving back and forth from side to side. Remove the stop bead and tie the beginning tail to the ending thread with a double square knot.

Variations

Two or three bead colors may be used, changing the color at the same place in each upward and downward weave, to create a gradual color shift. Small bugle beads (3 mm) and seed beads (size 15) make a narrow strip with an elegant, more tightly woven appearance. To make a shorter necklace, end the strip with an upward weave and attach a clasp.

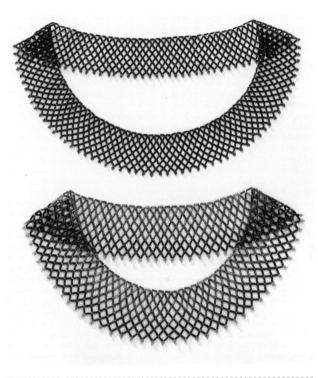

A Little Extra Security

Because bugles beads have sharp edges and the thread passes through them at an angle, there is a risk that one of them could cut the thread, especially at the top (neck edge) of the collar. For a little added security, stitch through the top bugle beads all the way around the neck edge. Using a doubled thread, knot and bury the tails.

YOU WILL NEED

- 20–30 g seed beads, size-11 or 10, single color

- seventy accent beads, 3 or 4 mm: crystals, glass pearls, shaped beads, or other

- beading thread, Nymo D, 6# Fireline, or equivalent

- beading needles: size 11 and 12

- clasp (or small button)

Use a size-11 needle for the majority of the weaving. Switch to a size 12 for going through beads that have lots of thread in them, such as when attaching the clasp.

Step Pictures for This Project

The step pictures for this project show the necklace in "teaching form," condensed so that both ends are visible in the picture. The color of the beads indicates which steps are complete (rose) and which step is currently active (purple). The stop bead is shown in each picture as reference to the starting point of the necklace and the direction of weaving in the current row.

SARAGURO LACE NECKLACE

Netting Worked Side to Side

The Saraguro people, an indigenous culture in Ecuador, have made and worn seed bead necklaces like this for more than 100 years. Their stunning beadwork includes a variety of designs and patterns for netted collars.

This version is woven from end to end, back and forth in rows. The first row forms the top band of the necklace. The remaining five rows form a series of loops, giving the work its graceful, lacey appearance. As beads are added, each new loop is secured to the row above it. In a manner similar to brick stitch (page 101), the needle goes under the thread between two beads in the row above, and then back through the last bead strung. This anchors each of the loops to the row above. The choice of beads makes it casual or dressy.

Tension

Check the tension frequently. Tight tension is very important for steps 1–4, which form row 1—the top band of the necklace. If the stitches loosen, it's possible to tighten the last two-stitch unit without much difficulty. If stitches farther back are loose, unravel the weaving back to the loose section and reweave it.

To avoid loose stitches, hold your work so your thumb and index finger cover the last completed stitch. Pull the thread and hold it tightly over your index finger. If you look at the tips of your finger and thumb, you should be able to see only a small bit of the last four beads. Generally it is possible to see which bead is needed for the next stitch. This tip refers only to row 1, steps 1–4.

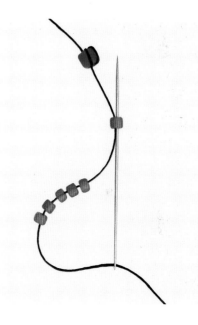

1   String and secure a stop bead, leaving an 8" (20 cm) tail. To begin row 1, string six seed beads and stitch back through the first bead with the needle pointing toward the stop bead. Pull the thread through, and tie the beading thread to the tail with a square knot. The stop bead is beyond the knot (not included with the other beads).

(continued)

Tension Change

Beginning with step 5, loosen the tension. Pull the thread enough so that the new bead sits next to the one above it, but is not so tight that a bead is forced between the beads of that row. After finishing a row, flip the work so you are always working left to right.

Reminder: Purple beads indicate the current step, and rose beads indicate completed steps. The photos show a short version of the necklace so that the transitions at both ends are visible.

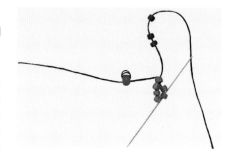

2 Hold your work with the tail thread at the top of your work. String three beads, skip the first bead, and go down through the next bead. Pull tightly so there is little or no thread showing.

3 String four beads and go up through the bead on top of the bead where the previous stitch exits. Continue to hold your work with the tail exiting the top left of your work.

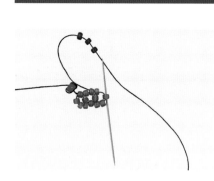

4 String three beads, skip the exit bead and the next bead, and go down through the third bead. Repeat steps 3–4 until the band is about the right length. Count the number of two-bead units at the top of the band by sevens. Add or remove the appropriate number of two-bead units so that the finished row is a multiple of seven units. On the last two-bead unit, sew through one extra bead so the thread exits between the bottom two beads of this unit.

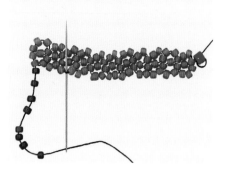

5 To begin row 2, string eight beads. Stitch under the thread between the two bottom beads of the third two-bead unit and then down through the last bead strung. This bead will secure the loop. It will be called the "anchor bead" for the rest of the project. For the remainder of the row, string seven beads for each loop. Continue to the end of the band to complete row 2. After anchoring the last seven beads in the row, stitch back through three more beads, exiting in the center of the last loop in row 2.

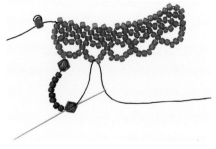

6 To begin row 3, string one accent bead, eight seed beads, and one accent bead. Skip three beads in the second loop in row 2 (not counting the anchor bead), sew under the thread between beads 3 and 4, and then go back through the accent bead and the next seed bead. In this row, the accent bead and one seed bead together form each anchor. For the rest of row 3, string seven seed beads and one accent bead and attach. Continue to the end of the row. In the last loop of row 3, go back through the last accent bead and two seed beads.

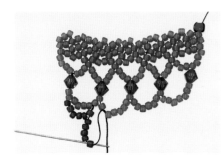

7 To begin row 4, string six beads. Skip four beads on the first loop of row 3 and attach through the anchor bead. String five beads and attach after the first bead of the second row 3 loop (not counting the anchor bead). String five more beads; skip four beads and attach the same way. Each loop in row 3 will have two loops anchored to it in row 4, doubling the total number of loops. Continue to string five beads for each loop and repeat to the end of the row. To anchor the last loop in this row, go back through two beads.

8 In row 5, each loop of beads will be attached between the middle two beads in the row 4 loops. To begin row 5, string twelve beads and attach them in the middle of the second loop of row 4. String five beads and attach them in the middle of the third loop. String five more beads and attach them to the fourth loop. String eleven beads and attach them to the fifth loop. Continue to the end of the row, repeating a pattern of 5-5-11 beads. At the end of the row, exit only the anchor bead.

Variations

A wide variety of beads can be used for the accent beads as long as the diameter is between 3 mm and 5 mm. Fire-polished beads are one way to add sparkle, or use Swarovski crystals for even more bling. Pearls add a feminine touch. Shaped beads like hearts, leaves, or flowers (with vertical holes) result in a less formal look.

This necklace is also pretty made in two (or more) colors such as pink for row 1, purple for rows 2 and 3, and pink for the remaining rows.

Rather than attaching a metal clasp, use a glass button with a beaded-loop closure.

Bracketing Crystals

The method shown here is the way the Saraguro women make this necklace. If you are using crystals for the accent beads, consider bracketing the accent beads (crystals) with seed beads, as shown on page 75. Bracketing crystals lessens the chance that their sharp edges will cut the thread.

9 To begin row 6, string eighteen beads and attach them between the two middle beads of the second loop in row 5. String two seed beads, one accent bead, and three seed beads. Skip the last three beads and go back up the accent bead. String three more beads and anchor to the third loop. Continue making these two

units, but use only seventeen beads for the rest of the big loops. For the last loop, do not go back through the last bead. Sew up through the end of each row, following along the outer edge to row 1.

10 To finish the necklace, use the thread from step 9 to attach one part of the clasp. Be sure to sew through several beads and knot securely. Repeat this step at least once more. For the other end of the necklace, you will need to add thread to attach the other half of the clasp. (For clasp attachment instructions, see page 75.)

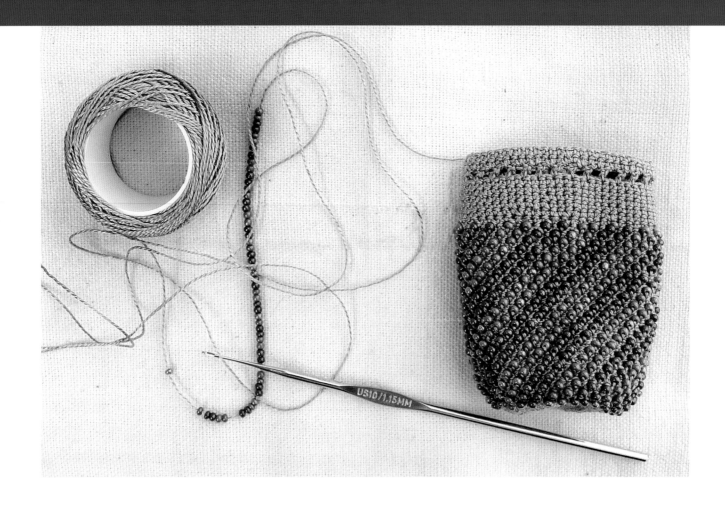

CROCHET WITH BEADS

Bead crochet first gained popularity in the mid-1800s, when extremely small beads were strung in a charted pattern on fine threads and then crocheted into fashionable handbags. It took many thousands of beads and countless hours of work to make a single bag. Some fine examples can be seen in museums and private collections. Intricate beaded patterns were also crocheted into bonnets, gloves, and other apparel.

Contemporary beaders make small crocheted amulet bags, such as the one pictured here. In addition beaded ropes, crocheted in a circular manner, as in the following project, are a popular core technique for making rope necklaces and lariats.

All bead crochet involves stringing beads onto the crochet thread first, either randomly or according to a charted pattern. Then, as the project is crocheted, a bead is slipped up the crochet thread next to the last stitch and held in place by the next stitch. When a bead is slipped forward with every stitch, the surface of the work will be covered with beads and the thread will be barely visible.

Warning: Memory Wire and Tools

Memory wire is hardened steel and therefore hard on tools. Using regular jewelry-making nippers and pliers on memory wire is likely to ruin the tools, causing nicks and dents in the working surfaces. Inexpensive tools from a thrift store can be used without worrying about damaging them.

The two approaches to bead embroidery may also be combined. For example, draw and plan colors for broad design areas, but bead improvisationally within these areas. For another mixed approach, develop a plan in your mind, but do not transfer the design to the beading surface. Allow the plan to shift however your mood and the beads suggest.

Scrutinizing Your Bead Embroidery

Often beaders become discouraged when they examine their bead embroidery stitches too closely. The lines aren't perfectly straight. The beads are uneven and may be turned on the side so the hole is up. There are places where the background surface shows between the beads. The beads look crowded in places, jumbled together.

All of these things are normal. Look at any bead embroidery in a gallery or museum and the beading will appear fine, maybe even perfect from a short distance away. Above, for example, is one of the author's pieces.

Look at it again, at closer range, checking for jumbled, bumpy, or crowded beads, and you will notice the same "imperfections" seen in your own work.

Of course, practice does help. As skill develops, you will have fewer and less obvious irregularities in your beading.

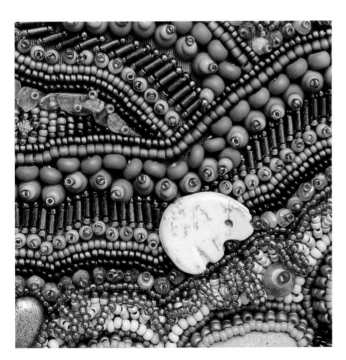

A SAMPLER OF
BEAD-EMBROIDERY STITCHES

The good news about learning bead embroidery is that there are only four basic stitches, all of which are easily learned. To complete the available palette, there are variations on the basic stitches and a few fancy stitches, fringes, bezels, and edge stitches.

To learn and practice the stitches, create a sampler—a single piece with all of the stitches available to you for reference. Gather a few beads and a favorite fabric. Give yourself a day or two to work through all the stitches. Even if you already know some of them, it's a good idea to include them on your sampler. A finished sampler is pictured to the left.

For ease of working with small beads, select colors that are matte and/or opaque rather than shiny and transparent. For a few of the stitches, it's nice to have the same color in different sizes. Choose medium- or light-value beads, rather than black or very dark beads. The beads will show better on a lighter value fabric in a solid or a subtle print than on a dark or bold print fabric.

Draw a 5" (13 cm) square centered on the stabilizer. Pin the stabilizer, with the drawn square facing out, to the wrong side of the fabric. Using a thread color that can be seen easily on the fabric, baste along the outline of the square to prepare the sampler for beading (see page 137).

Unless directed otherwise, practice the stitches anywhere on the sampler. Some people like to keep the stitches separate and write on the fabric to indicate what they are. Some enjoy playing with design as they practice, creating an artful piece. For a few of the stitch variations, there will be suggestions about where to place them.

YOU WILL NEED

- 15 g seed beads, size 15, g each of three colors

- 30 g seed beads, size 11, 10 g each of three colors (OK to substitute size-10 beads)

- 10 g seed beads, size 8, 5 g each of two colors

- 5 g seed beads, size 6, one color

- 5 g bugle beads, size 3 (short), one color

- six sequins, any size and color

- four glass beads, one each: leaf, drop, donut or ring, disk or roundel (OK to substitute stone beads)

- one cabochon, stone or glass, approximately 8 x 12 mm

- 6" (15 cm) square cotton fabric, quilting weight, print or solid

- 6" (15 cm) square of stabilizer paper, acid-free

- beading needles, size 10, 11, and 12

- beading thread, Nymo or equivalent, size D

SEED STITCH

Bead-Embroidery Sampler

The seed stitch is the simplest stitch of the four, yet has many useful variations. It is used to attach sequins and other shaped beads such as disks. It becomes the top bead in short and tall stacks, which in turn can be used to make textural forms such as barnacles, ruffles, and beaded bezels, shown later in this chapter.

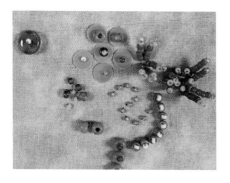
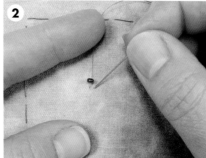
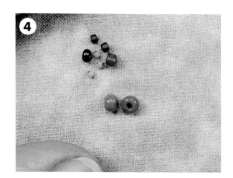

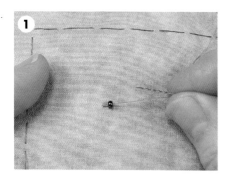

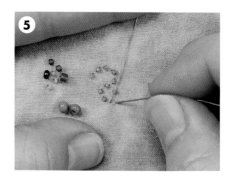

Basic Seed Stitch

The most basic form of seed stitch involves sewing one bead at a time, making a cluster of dots on the beading surface, much like French knots in thread embroidery.

1 Stitch to the surface. Pick up one bead and slide it down the thread to the surface.

2 Stitch to the back about one bead's width away from where the thread exits on the surface.

3 Repeat steps 1–2 several times, making a cluster of beads. Use beads of varying sizes. Try a different version of the same stitch. Rather than sewing to the back a bead's width away, sew to the back in the same place where the thread exits.

4 Notice that the bead is turned now so that both the hole and the thread are visible. This is an optional way to do seed stitch.

5 Using size-15 beads make a dotted line of seed stitch beads in the shape of an "S." Leave a space of about a bead's width between each of the beads. Turn the sampler, orienting it as needed for ease of stitching the design.

LAZY STITCH

Bead-Embroidery Sampler

The lazy stitch is a short, straight line of beads sewn on as a single unit with one stitch. It is the characteristic stitch used by some Native American tribes, see the picture to the right. It is especially useful for making patterned borders and for filling small spaces.

Basic Lazy Stitch

In its basic form, this stitch is worked in a column, from side to side, designated A for the start and B for the end of each row.

1 Stitch to the surface in a new area. String four size-11 beads. Determine the direction of the column's rows and lay the thread against the fabric in this direction. Hold the thread in place with your nondominant hand.

2 Using the needle as a pusher, gently scoot the beads along the thread toward the A side.

3 At the end of the column, insert the needle into the fabric, straight down, perpendicular to the fabric. The beads should lie flat on the fabric. If there is a small hump, the beads are too crowded on the thread, which could be caused either by inserting the needle at a slant toward the A side or by pushing the beads too hard against the A side in step 2.

4 Stitch to the surface on the A side about a bead's width away from the start of row 1. Repeat steps 2 and 3 for the second row in the column. The two rows should be parallel and touching each other with no gap between the rows.

5 Repeat step 4 several more times. Finding the correct place to come to the surface on the A side and keeping the rows flat takes a little practice. Keep adding rows to the column until it looks satisfactory.

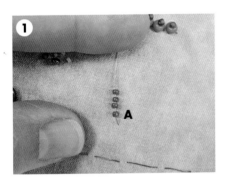

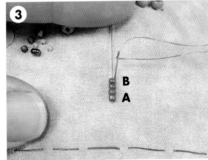

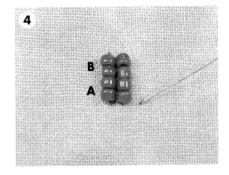

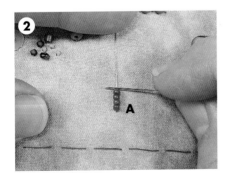

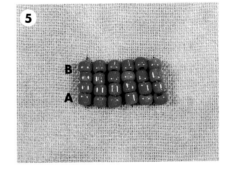

Lazy-Stitch Borders

Use lazy stitch to create a border design around a piece of beadwork. Practice it along one edge of the sampler. Designate the basted line around the sampler as the A side of the column. The pattern shown below is quite simple. Feel free to substitute any bead loom or cross-stitch pattern (up to six beads wide).

1 Stitch to the surface anywhere along the basted guide on one edge of the sampler. Work with two colors of size-11 beads, P (purple) and G (green). String 5P, and stitch to the back on side B.

2 Stitch to the surface on the A side about a bead's width away from the previous stitch. String 2P, 1G, and 2P, and stitch to the back on the B side.

3 Stitch to the surface on the A side about a bead's width away from the previous stitch. String 1P, 3G, and 1P, and stitch to the back on the B side.

4 Repeat step 2.

5 Repeat step 1.

6 Repeat steps 2–5 several times, making a patterned border along the edge of the sampler.

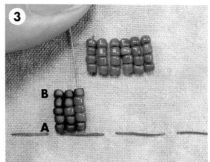

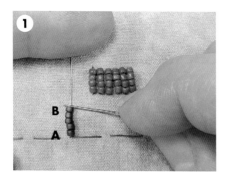

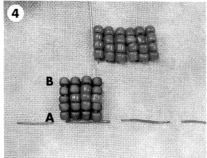

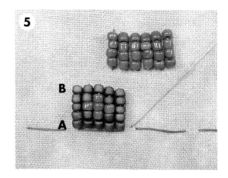

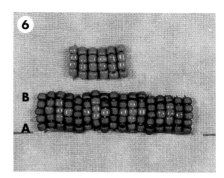

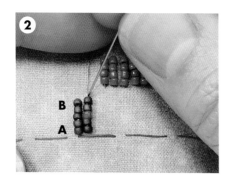

Lazy-Stitch Patchwork

This variation of lazy stitch creates an interesting background and subtle texture. When worked in a single color, it looks like a basket weave. When worked in multiple colors, it looks like patchwork

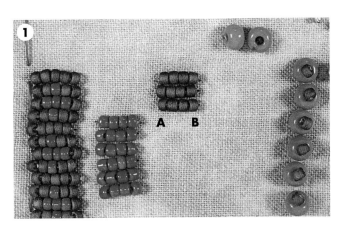

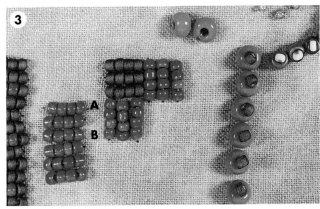

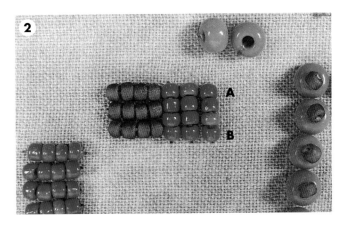

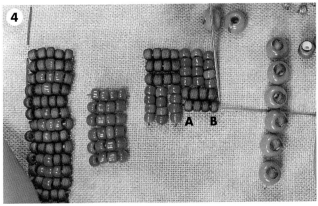

1 Following the steps for basic lazy stitch, make three horizontal rows of size-11 beads. Each row will be three beads long. It should look like a small square of beads in a single color.

2 Using a different color of size-11 beads, and changing the A and B sides to top and bottom, make three vertical rows of three beads each. This makes a second square of beads next to the first, with the beads lying along a vertical rather than horizontal axis.

3 Use the same color of size-11 beads, and make a third square of beads under the first square, with the beads lying along a vertical axis.

4 Complete the patchwork block by making a fourth square next to the third with the original color of beads lying along a horizontal axis.

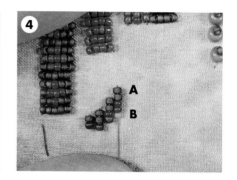

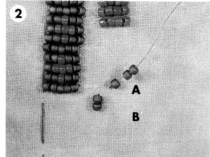

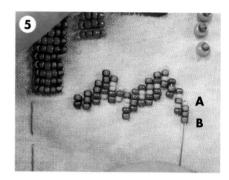

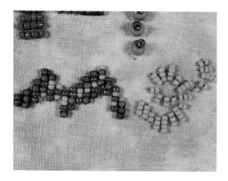

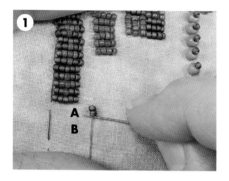

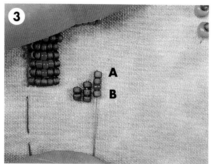

Lazy-Stitch Pathway

This ribbon-like variation of the lazy stitch can be made with beads of mixed sizes. Unlike the regular rows starting in a straight column on the A side, both the A and B points shift to create irregular rows of different lengths. To practice this variation, make both a jagged and a looped pathway.

1 Jagged Lazy-Stitch Pathway
   To make the jagged pathway, use up to six beads for each row. Mix the sizes and colors if you like. Keep the rows parallel and touching each other, as in the basic lazy stitch. Stitch to the surface anywhere on the fabric. String two beads. Determine the direction of the pathway and the B point perpendicular to the path. Stitch to the back.

2 The new A point will be slightly higher than the previous A point, but still a bead's width away from the previous row. String three beads, lay them against the previous row, and stitch to the back.

3 Shift the A point upward again, string four beads, lay them against the previous row, and stitch to the back.

4 Shift the A point upward again, string five beads, lay them against the previous row, and stitch to the back.

5 Begin now to move the A point downward. Stitch several more rows parallel to the previous rows, changing the number of beads and lowering the A point for each row. Repeat steps 1–5, changing the number of beads in the rows to create an irregular pathway.

5 String five more beads, and repeat steps 2–4. Continue backstitching toward the center of the spiral. When the spiral is tight, string fewer beads with each stitch until at the center of the spiral you may need to make the stitch with only two or three beads. Knot on the back.

6 Use the "magic trick" (see page 157) to smooth the line of the spiral, stitching through all of the beads in the line.

7 Follow steps 2–6 to bead the outline of the heart, starting at the lower point. For the backstitch just before the center top of the heart, select narrower or wider beads so the line will end just before the center point. Stitch to the back and knot.

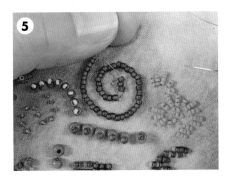

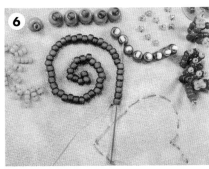

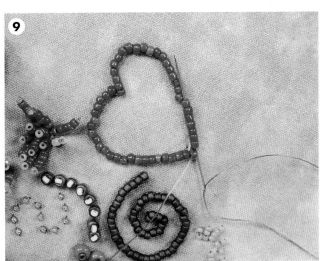

8 Stitch to the surface right at the center point, and begin beading the other side of the heart shape following steps 3–4. Knot on the back.

9 Use the "magic trick" to smooth the heart shape. Stitch to the surface and then through all of the beads on one side of the heart. Stitch to the back and knot. Repeat for the other side of the heart.

COUCHING STITCH

Bead-Embroidery Sampler

The couching stitch is used to tack a long line of beads around a disc or cabochon, to make minor adjustments to lines of backstitched beads, and to tack down lines of lazy stitched beads.

Couching Beads around a Disk

To practice couching a line of beads around a rounded element, use the disk that was attached previously with the seed stitch (see page 150).

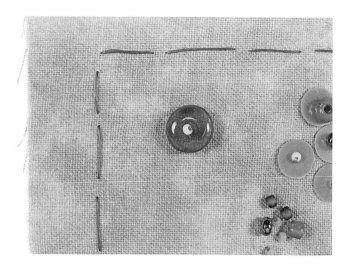

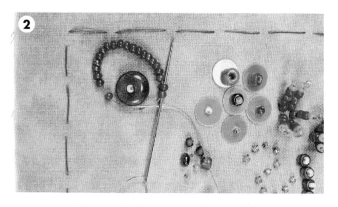

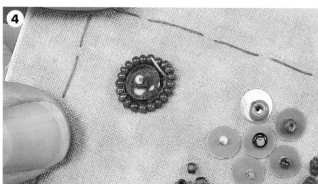

1 Stitch to the surface next to the disk. String on as many beads as it takes to circle the disk.

2 Stitch through the first two beads again.

3 Between the second and third bead, stitch straight down to the back.

4 Stitch to the surface, positioning the needle so it comes up between the disc and the line of beads about four beads farther around the line.

7 Picot Edge Stitch
Stitch to the surface along the fold line, ¼" (6 mm) to the right of the last single bead edge stitch. String three beads. Stitch across the fold line from back to front, about two bead's width away from the starting point.

8 Stitch through the third bead from the underside, close to the fabric, upward.

9 String two beads. Stitch across the fold line from back to front, about two bead's width away from the previous stitch.

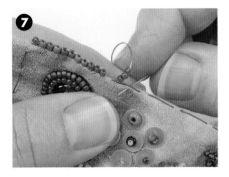

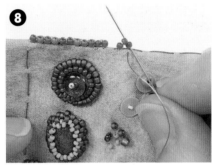

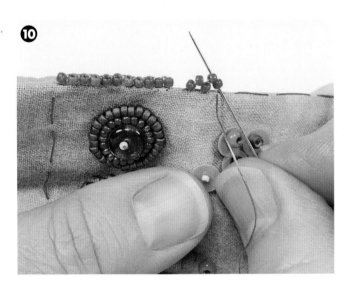

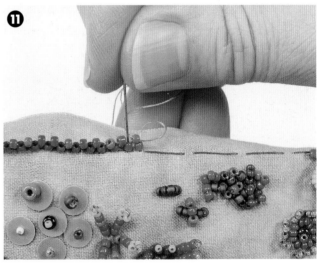

10 Stitch through the second of the beads just added from the underside, close to the fabric, upward.

11 Repeat steps 9–10 several times. There should be a definite point for each stitch. If the work looks flat, sew across the fold line closer to the previous stitch. If the work looks like a solid wall, sew across the fold line a little farther away from the previous stitch. To end, after step 11, stitch backward through the second and third to the last bead. Stitch to the underside of the fold, and knot.

(continued)

12 Whipped Edge Stitch

Stitch to a starting point which is ¼" (6 mm) to the right of the last picot edge stitch, and about ¼" (6 cm) lower than the fold.

13 String seven beads. Stitch across the fold, back to front, about one bead's width beyond the starting point and ¼" (6 mm) lower than the fold.

14 Repeat step 13 several times. The whipped lines of beads should touch each other, completely hiding the fold line. The beads should wrap over the fold without a gap between the middle bead and the fold. If it looks too loose or tight, try adjusting the number of the beads in each stitch or moving the starting point up or down a slight distance. To end, stitch to inside of the fold from the back and knot.

15 Continue making edge stitches along the fold line. Try other sizes of beads and color combinations.

Edge-Stitch Tips

Rounding the arc of a corner with edge stitches generally requires tighter spacing. To round an inside corner, spread the stitches apart a little.

Join two pieces, such as the front and back of a pouch, together with an edge stitch. When stitching across the fold, be sure to catch the edge of both pieces. In the same way, stitch a lining or backing to a piece of bead embroidery using an edge stitch. When a section of edging is complete, make a small knot under the last bead, stitch between the layers for about 1" (2.5 cm), exit on the surface, pull slightly, and cut the thread.

Use an edge stitch to decorate a flat seam, for example in a quilt block. Fold the piece along the seam, work the edge stitch along the fold, and then open the piece out flat. The edge stitch will be a straight, raised line.

When a paper stabilizer is used, it can be torn away at the basting line before working the edge stitches. "Press" the fold by pinching tightly with your fingers. Optional: Remove the basted stitch guide prior to working the edge stitches.

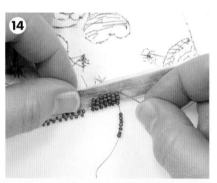

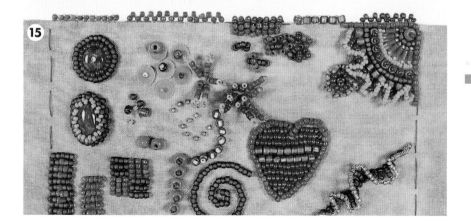

FRINGES

Bead-Embroidery Sampler

Fringes add movement and texture to bead embroidery. They offer a great opportunity to feature special or unique beads. Some designs call for a symmetrical, repeating pattern of fringes. At other times it may be fun to mix a variety of fringe techniques in an asymmetrical arrangement.

Any of the following fringes may be made short and used as surface fringe or surface texture. Fringes may also be couched to the beading surface.

Among many fringe methods, these represent the most commonly used types: basic, diamond-point, loop, drop-bead, branch, and twisted fringe.

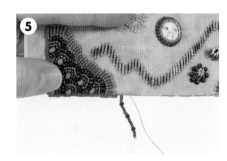

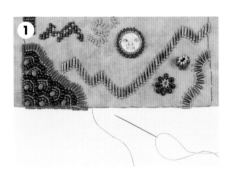

1 You can choose where to place the fringes on the sampler. Either put them along the bottom edge with the seam allowance folded to the back at the basting line. Or put them anywhere on the surface of the beaded sampler. Because fringes are vulnerable to getting caught, make a knot on the back after each fringe. Use any beads, including mixed sizes if you wish, except where directed otherwise. Make a knot at the end of a single thread, and stitch to the surface where the first fringe will be placed.

2 Basic Fringe
String about 1½" (4 cm) of beads for the trunk of the fringe. String one size-15 bead for the anchor bead. Skip the anchor bead, and stitch through the trunk to the back.

3 Tension
Keep in mind that thread always stretches a little over time, especially when there is weight on it. The heavier the fringe, the more the thread will stretch. Grasp the anchor bead in one hand and the needle in the other. Pull upward on the needle,

while maintaining slight downward tension on the anchor bead. This should pull the fringe snug to the beading surface. It's the beader's choice about how tight to pull the fringe. Flexible fringes look good; yet the stretch factor should also be a consideration.

4 If placing the fringe along the fold, knot inside the fold. If placing the fringe on the surface, stitch to the back and knot.

5 Position the needle for the next fringe.

(continued)

6 Diamond-Point Fringe

String beads for the trunk. String four size-11 beads for the diamond point. Skip the last three beads, and stitch through the remainder of the beads to the inside of the fold.

7 To adjust the tension, grasp the middle of the three beads at the end of the fringe in one hand and pull upward with the needle in the other hand (as in step 3). Adjust the bottom four beads as needed to form a diamond shape. Knot inside the fold and position the needle for the next fringe.

8 Loop Fringe

String four size-11 beads and one size-6 bead for the trunk. String about 2" (5 cm) of size-15 beads. Stitch through the center of the ring. With the ring positioned along the size-15 beads, stitch through the trunk to the inside of the fold.

9 Adjust the tension, knot, and position the needle for the next fringe as in steps 3–5. Note: The ring is optional. The loop fringe can be used to hang a charm from the end of a fringe.

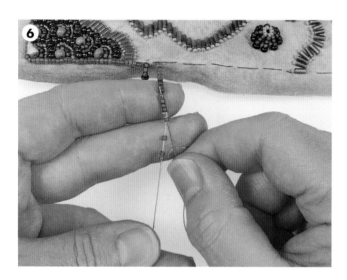

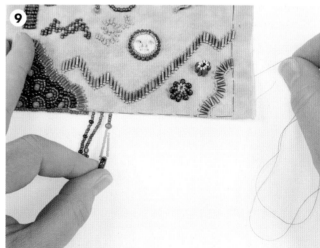

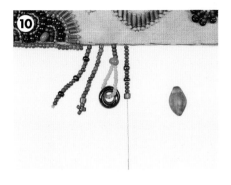

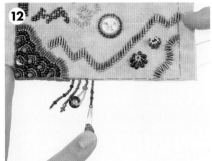

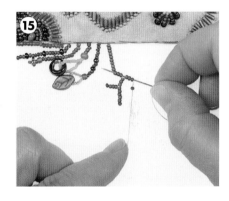

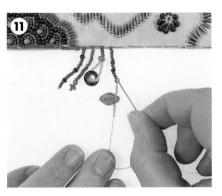

10 Drop-Bead Fringe

Any bead with a hole across the top, such as a drop, leaf, lentil, or flower may be used at the end of a fringe. String beads for the trunk.

11 String six size-15 beads, the drop bead, and six more size-15 beads. Stitch through the trunk to the back.

12 Adjust the tension, knot, and position the needle for the next fringe as in steps 3–5. Note: The drop bead fringe can be used to hang a charm from the end of a fringe. Depending on the length of the hole at the top of the drop bead, increase or decrease the number of size-15 beads on either side so that it hangs freely.

13 Branch Fringe

Also called "kinky fringe," this fringe can have many branches, twigs, and twigs-on-twigs. A very full branch fringe may be couched to the surface to resemble bushes or thick vegetation.

Practice this fringe using size-11 beads only. String a sufficient number of beads for the desired length of the fringe (the trunk). String one anchor bead. Slide all the beads snug against the beading surface. Stitch back through five beads of the trunk and exit.

14 To make the first branch, string four beads. Skip the last bead, and stitch back through the other three beads and upward into the trunk. Exit about three beads beyond the branch.

15 Adjust the tension to ensure the trunk and the branch are snug. Repeat step 14 to make a second branch.

(continued)

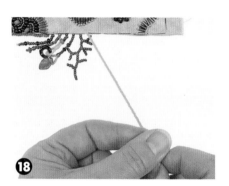

16 Make a Branch with a Twig

String six beads, skip the last bead, stitch back through three beads, and exit. Adjust the tension. To make a twig, string three beads, skip the last bead, stitch back through the branch and upward into the trunk. Exit about three beads beyond the branch and twig. Pull the fringe snug and adjust the tension.

17 Continue to work up the trunk, making several branches with twigs along the way. Stitch to the back and knot. Note: Each branch and twig on this fringe could have a diamond, loop, or other fancy ending.

18 Twisted Fringe

The beads in the trunk of this fringe twist around on themselves to make a rope-like fringe. The most important requirement is that the thread must fill the holes of the beads.

Use a doubled thread for this fringe and size-15 beads. String about 4" (10 cm) of beads. Slide the beads snug against the beading surface. Grasp the doubled thread just beyond the last bead, and twist it repeatedly in one direction. Dampen your fingers if necessary.

19 To test the twist, hold the midpoint of the strung beads with one hand, and place the needle end of the beads next to the start of the fringe.

20 Let go of the midpoint to see if it twists into a rope. If it does not, twist the thread more times and try again. When the strands twist, keep holding the thread at the end of the beads, and at the same time stitch to the back. Pull snug and knot.

Fringes Getting in the Way?

When beading on the surface after completing fringes, the beading thread gets caught and tangled in the fringes. An easy fix for this problem is to wrap the fringes in a scrap of fabric and baste it closed, as shown below. Another fix is to wrap the fringes in tinfoil, scrunching it tight.

21

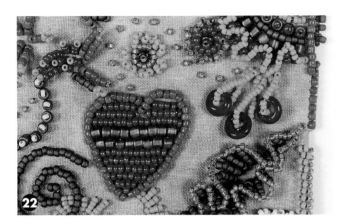

22

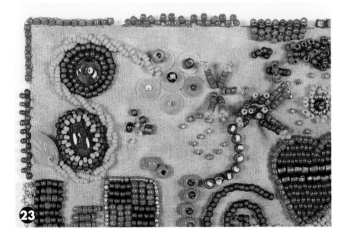

23

Tips for Making Fringes

"Press" the fold by pinching tightly with your fingers. Optional: Remove the basted stitch guide and the margin of paper stabilizer prior to working the fringes.

For an evenly spaced line of fringes, use a ruler and fine-tip pen to mark a dot on the starting point for each fringe.

To place fringes along the finished edge of a piece, string the trunk and anchor of the fringe, stitch back up through the trunk, and stitch through the edge of the piece at the top of the fringe. Secure each fringe by making a knot at the top of the fringe. To make the knot, take another small stitch through the finished edge of the piece, pull the thread until there is a little loop showing, stitch through the loop two times, and slowly pull the knot tight. Stitch between the layers of the piece to position the needle for the next fringe.

Bugle beads, crystals, or other beads with sharp edges around the hole may be used in fringes. However, it is best to bracket these types of beads with a seed bead on either side (see page 75).

Use these same fringe designs and methods on woven or strung bead projects. The only difference is how the fringe is attached to the project. In woven projects, it is wise to secure the thread back into the body of weaving between each fringe.

21 Practice making fringes along the bottom edge of the sampler. Use various bead sizes and color combinations.

22 Make several short loop fringes on the surface of the sampler (see steps 8–9).

23 Make a twisted fringe on the surface of the sampler, and couch it in place. Couch over the curves of the twisted line of beads where they touch the beading surface. Twisted fringe may be couched to a doll's head to represent curls or a braid.

CREATIVE SPIRIT ATC
Improvisational Bead Embroidery on Fabric

Pick a theme and play with the concept of beading improvisationally! Make an artist trading card (ATC) to trade with another artist or to display on a mini-easel. The idea here is to practice working without a plan, to select fabric and beads without knowing in advance how, or even if, you will use them.

Some possible themes are friendship, family, marriage, spirituality, one of the seasons of the year, a favorite

place, or an enjoyable activity. The theme underlying the example here is "the creative spirit" or muse. Choose your own theme, tuck the thought of it in the back of your mind, and start beading. It's better not to think about how exactly you can illustrate the theme. Let it come forward from your subconscious. This will happen quite naturally as you let go of the need to control and plan the piece.

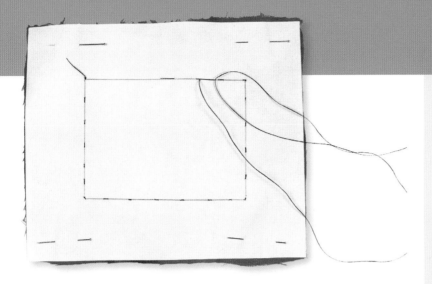

1   In the center of the paper stabilizer, measure and draw a rectangle 2½" x 3½" (6.4 x 8.9 cm), the standard ATC size. With the drawing side up, place this paper stabilizer on the wrong side of your fabric and baste along the drawn line. Use a contrasting color of thread and make the stitches long on the fabric side and short on the paper side, so you can easily see this basted guide on the fabric side. If the fabric frays easily, turn under ¼" (6 mm) along the edges and baste.

YOU WILL NEED

- 4½" x 5½" (11.4 x 14 cm) quilting-weight fabric, print or solid
- acid-free paper stabilizer, cut to 4½" x 5½" (11.4 x 14 cm)
- assorted seed beads in sizes 15, 11, and 8
- bugle beads, small, one color
- assorted shaped beads, charms, buttons, found objects
- beading thread, Nymo or equivalent, size D
- beading needle, size 11 or 12
- heavy cardstock, cut to 2½" x 3½" (6.4 x 8.9 cm) (or blank ATC card)
- synthetic suede (Ultrasuede Light or equivalent), cut to 2½" x 3½" (6.4 x 8.9 cm), for backing

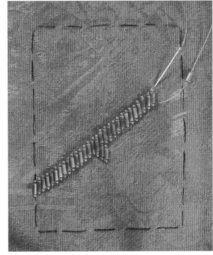

2   Select a variety of beads, buttons, and charms that you might want to use for this project. Store them in a bag or box for the duration of the project. Since you will actually use only a small percentage of the items, there is no need to be concerned if these items are right for the theme of the project, if they match the fabric, or if they go with each other. Keeping the subject of the ATC in the back of your mind, simply pick beads that seem attractive or compelling to you.

3   The thought of sewing beads on a blank fabric with no plan may seem daunting. A good way to get over that hurdle is to divide the fabric into smaller sections. Use bugle bead pathways, lines of short stacks, or backstitching for this purpose. The lines can be straight or curved.

(continued)

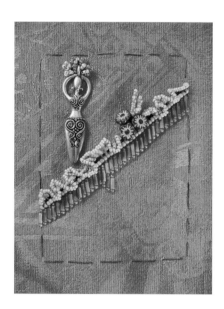

4 Play with the lines a little, adding more beads along them. In this example, a line of backstitched beads, a ruffle, and some flower beads accentuate the line formed by the bugle bead pathway.

5 When beading along the lines begins to seem uninteresting, choose one of the areas created by the lines and find something in your project box to put there. Stitch it on. Play with it a little, adding beads around or near it.

6 If you begin to feel stuck, not knowing what to add next, move to one of the unbeaded areas, and add something there. Or, further divide one of the areas with another bugle-bead pathway.

7 Sometimes, it feels right to define the ATC borders with a line of backstitched beads, as in this example. Other methods for defining the borders include using a line of short stacks or a narrow border made with lazy stitch. Let some of the interior beading extend to the edge, so the border line is broken in a few places.

5 Pass the needle and thread over the top of the line of beads. Stitch to the back so that the thread crosses over the thread between the two closest beads in the line. This is a couching stitch. Allow couching stitches to be loose. If they are pulled too tight, the couched line of beads will not be smooth.

6 Stitch to the surface about four beads farther around the line, positioning the needle so it comes up between the disk and the line of beads. Repeat step 5.

7 Continue couching around the circle, spacing the couching stitches evenly.

8 For practice, couch a second line of beads around the first one, following steps 1–7.

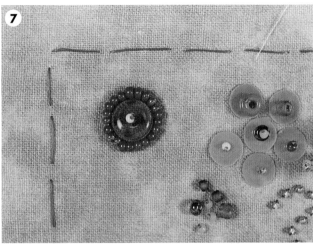

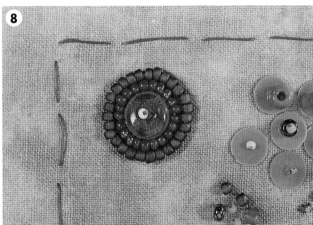

The "magic trick" (see page 157) may help to smooth the line of beads. Note that the more beads in the line, the more difficult it is to keep the line smooth. To make a third line of beads around the first two, backstitching the line, rather than couching it, will produce more satisfactory results.

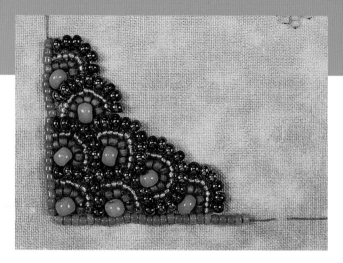

Couching Beads in a Fan Pattern

Practice the fan pattern in the corner bordered by lines of backstitched beads.

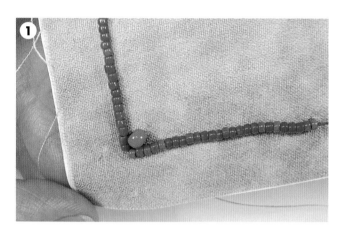

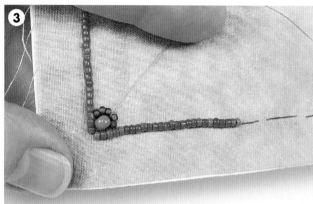

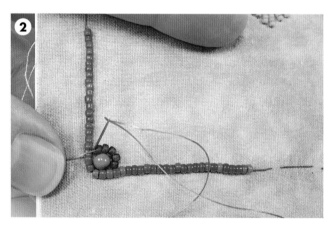

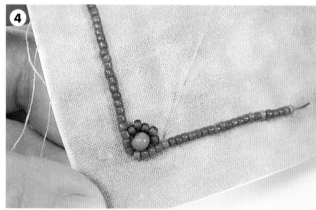

1 Stitch to the surface in the corner. Use the seed stitch (see page 146) to sew a single, size-6 bead in the corner.

2 Stitch to the surface where the size-6 bead and the line of beads meet. String enough size-11 beads to fit around the size-6 bead to the adjacent line of beads. Stitch straight down to the back.

3 Stitch to the surface between the size-6 bead and the arc of beads around it at about the midpoint of the arc. Cross over the arc of size-11 beads, and stitch to the back. This couches the arc in place.

4 Stitch to the surface next to the last bead of the arc.

5 String enough size-15 beads to fit around the first arc. Stitch to the back at the end of the second arc. Couch the second arc in two evenly spaced places.

6 Couch a third arc of beads around the first two. Use any size beads. This completes the first fan.

7 Stitch to the surface at one of the corners formed by the arc and the border line. Repeat steps 1–7 to make a second fan.

8 Stitch to the surface in any of the corners formed by a fan-to-fan or fan-to-border intersection. Repeat steps 1–7 to make a third fan. Continue making fans to fill the corner.

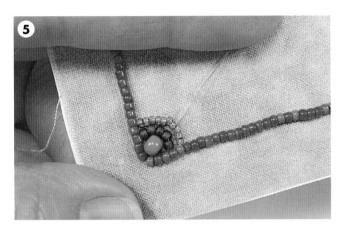

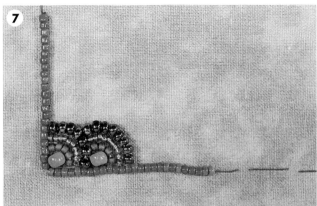

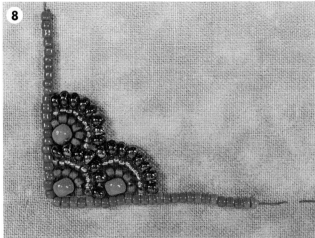

Couching Beads to Fill Spaces

The most common use of the couching stitch in bead embroidery is to fill small spaces. To practice this, fill the beaded outline of a heart (see page 159) using a combination of lazy stitch and couching.

1 Stitch to the surface inside the heart slightly to the right of the lower point. Use seed stitch (see page 146) to sew one bead in the point.

2 Stitch to the surface on the right side, next to the bead in the point. String two or three beads, enough to cross to the left side, and stitch straight down to the back. This is lazy stitch (see page 151).

3 Stitch to the surface on the right side, next to the row below. String three to six beads, enough to cross to the left side, and stitch straight down to the back. This is the second row of lazy stitch.

4 Continue making rows of lazy stitch until the number of beads in the row is seven or more. At this point, couch the row of beads in the center.

5 Continue couching rows of beads to fill the heart outline, until the top center point is reached.

6 Use lazy stitch to fill each of the top bumps of the heart shape.

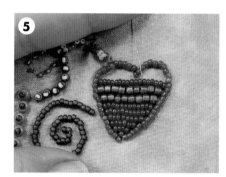

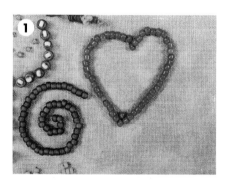

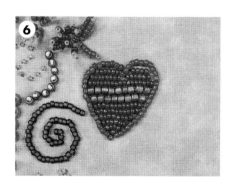

Filling Large Areas

When filling areas larger than 2" (5 cm) across, it gives a smoother appearance to backstitch the rows of beads rather than couch them.

Raven Moon (page 188)

Creative Spirit (page 184)

What makes the difference between one piece of bead embroidery and another (for example, between a Native American dress and a beaded wedding gown) isn't the technique so much as other factors. These include the predominance of one stitch over the others, the amount of beading surface covered, the design, and the specific beads used. For this reason, once the basic stitches are learned, anything is possible; any desired style may be achieved!

For example, take a look at these two ATC projects. *Raven Moon* is solidly beaded, representational, and worked primarily in backstitch. On the other hand, *Creative Spirit* is partially beaded, abstract, and worked in a variety of stitches. The effects they create are quite different.

Bead-Embroidery Sampler

You have completed the four basic stitches and a number of variations. With just these stitches you can create many different styles of bead embroidery. In addition, there are four fancy stitches that may be fun to add to your sampler. They are bumps, bugle-bead pathways, ruffles, and barnacles.

Bumps

Tall, short, and overlapping bead bumps add texture to bead embroidery. They can be used to simulate flowing water, vegetation, bark, flower petals, fur, and other textured surfaces when beading a realistic picture.

1   A bump is like a lazy stitch (see page 151), except that it does not lie flat against the fabric. In an unbeaded area of the sampler, stitch to the surface, string five size-11 beads, and stitch to the back about one bead's width away. This is a tall bump.

2   Close by, repeat step 1, except stitch to the back about four bead's width away. This is a flat bump.

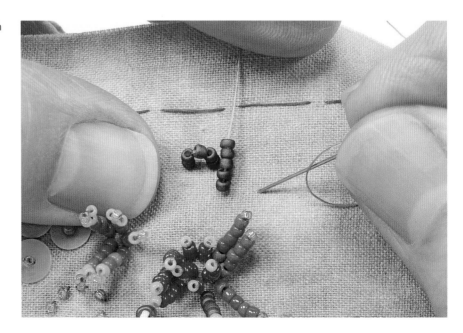

3 Repeat step 1, positioning the tall bump so it crosses over the flat bump. A series of crossing bumps can be made to look like tree bark or flowing water.

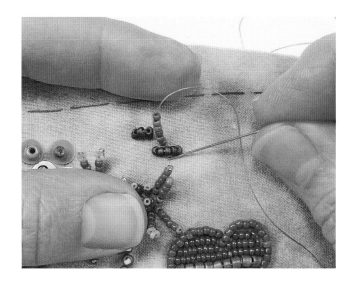

4 Stitch to the surface, string three size-11 beads, and stitch to the back about one bead's width away. This is a small bump. Orienting them in different directions, make a cluster of small bumps, grouped together.

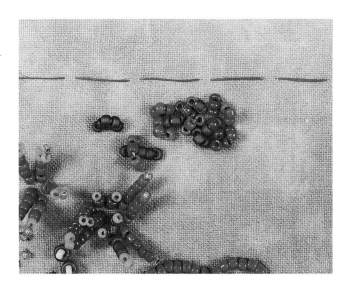

5 Use bumps to make a realistic-looking flower. Make a short stack for the center (see page 147). Couch a ring of beads around the center stack (see page 160). Make a series of tall, five-bead bumps around the ring to look like petals.

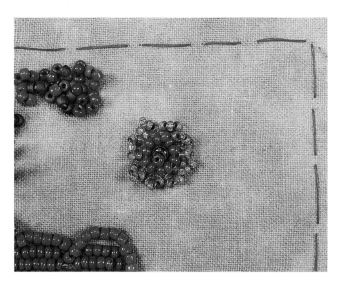

Bugle-Bead Pathways

Similar to lazy-stitch pathways (see page 154), this stitch produces a wide, flowing line of beads. Use it to divide the beading surface into small areas or to create obvious lines in a design. Bracketing bugle beads on each end with a seed bead provides a relatively safe way to use bugle beads, which often have sharp, thread-cutting ends.

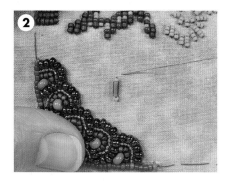

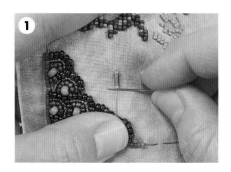

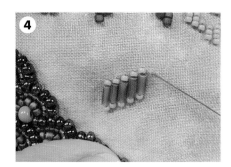

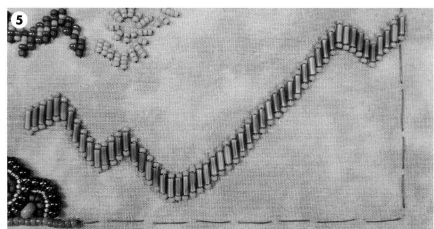

1 Staggered Bugle-Bead Pathway
Stitch to the surface in an unbeaded area. To practice this stitch, use size-15 beads and bugle beads. String one seed bead, one bugle bead, and one seed bead for each stitch. Lay the thread on the fabric perpendicular to the direction of the pathway. Scoot the beads toward the starting point, and stitch straight downward to the back at the end of the row.

2 Stitch to the surface about a bead's width from the start of the previous row and about a bead's width higher.

3 String one seed bead, one bugle bead, and one seed bead. Scoot the beads toward the starting point, and stitch straight downward to the back at the end of the row. Keep the rows parallel and touching each other. Repeat steps 2–3 several times.

4 Stitch to the surface about a bead's width from the start of the previous row and about a bead's width lower.

5 String one seed bead, one bugle bead, and one seed bead. Scoot the beads toward the starting point, and stitch straight downward to the back at the end of the row. Make several more rows, each starting a little lower than the previous row. Repeat steps 2–3 several more times. Notice that the rows of beads touch each other and that no fabric shows between them. Continue making staggered rows of beads, raising or lowering the starting point of each row to shape the pathway.

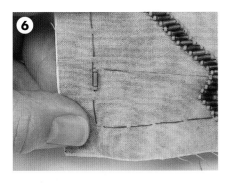

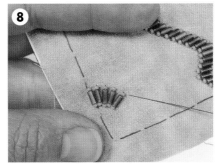

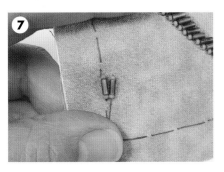

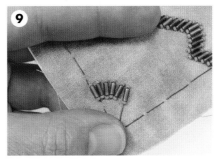

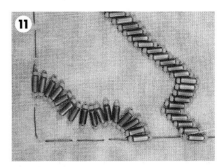

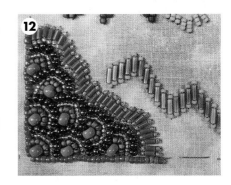

6 Fanned Bugle-Bead Pathways
Continue with the same pathway or start the fanned method in a new location. Follow step 1 to make the first row of the fanned pathway. Stitch to the surface about two beads' width from the start of the previous row.

7 String one seed bead, one bugle bead, and one seed bead. Lay the thread on the fabric so that it is about a bead's width from the end of the previous row. Scoot the beads toward the starting point, and stitch straight downward to the back at the end of the row.

Make several more fanned rows. Notice that the beads fan outward from the ending points of the rows and that the fabric shows between them.

8 To fan the rows in the opposite direction, begin the next row about one bead's width from the previous row.

9 String the beads for the row. Lay the thread on the fabric so that it is about two beads' width from the end of the previous row. Scoot the beads toward toward the starting point, and stitch straight downward to the back at the end of the row.

10 Repeat steps 8–9 several times.

11 Continue making rows, fanning either the top or bottom of each row to shape the pathway.

12 A fanned bugle-bead pathway makes an attractive row in the couched fan pattern (see page 162). Add one to the corner section already completed.

Ruffles

Ruffles add both texture and a sense of movement to bead embroidery. Like many stitch variations, ruffles begin with lines of short and tall stacks (see pages 147 and 148).

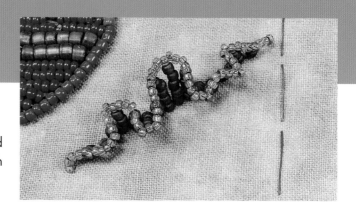

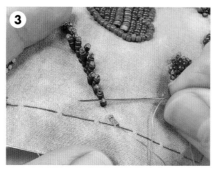

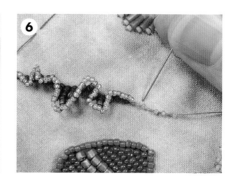

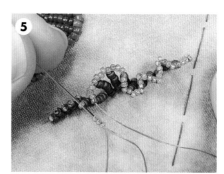

1 In an unbeaded area, make a straight or curved line of stacks. Use size-11 beads for the trunk and a size-15 bead for the top bead of each stack. Begin the line by using only two beads in the stack (including the top bead). For the next two stacks, use three beads.

2 Continue making stacks, gradually increasing the height to six beads tall (including the top bead). After making several six-bead stacks, gradually decrease the height of the stacks, back to two beads. After completing the final two-bead stack, knot on the back.

3 Stitch to the surface just beyond the final two-bead stack. String four size-15 seed beads, and stitch through the top bead of the end stack.

4 String three size-15 beads, and stitch through the top bead of the next stack.

5 Repeat step 4 along the whole line of stacks, adding either two or three beads between each of the stacks. The more beads added between top beads, the more fluffy the ruffle will become. As a rule of thumb, add fewer beads than the number of beads in the stacks.

6 At the end of the line, after joining the top bead of the last stack, string four beads, and stitch to the back just beyond the first stack. Pull the thread snug and knot.

Barnacles

Like the shells of the small crustaceans for which they are named, beaded barnacles make an intriguing raised surface element that can suggest a volcano, the center of a flower, or a cityscape. Use a barnacle as a cage to hold a special little bead. Depending on the beads used and the spacing, it can taper inward drastically or be more straight-sided, like a tower.

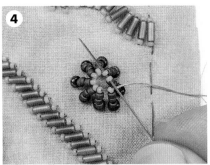

5 Repeat steps 1–4 to make a second barnacle. This time, use four size-11 beads topped by a size-15 bead for each stack. Make the stacks right next to each other, with no space between them. Notice how changing the spacing and bead size alters the look of the barnacle.

1 Make a small circle of tall stacks (see page 148), with the unbeaded fabric in the center measuring about ½" (1.3 cm) in diameter. For each stack, use one size-8 bead, three size-11 beads, and one size-15 bead. The top bead of each stack is size 15. Space the stacks a short distance apart around the ring.

2 After completing the final stack, knot on the back. Stitch through the fabric and the beads in the first stack.

3 Join the top beads of all the stacks all the way around.

4 Stitch through the top bead of the first and second stack a second time. Stitch downward through the second stack to the back. Pull the thread snug and knot.

BEZELS

Bead-Embroidery Sampler

A bezel is a thin, slanted "wall" used to enclose a cabochon and hold it in place on a surface. A cabochon is a flat-bottomed, dome-topped piece of stone, glass, or other material. In a ring, for example, a stone cabochon would be held in place with a metal bezel. In bead embroidery, there are many cabochons or cabochon-like elements that may be attached with a beaded bezel.

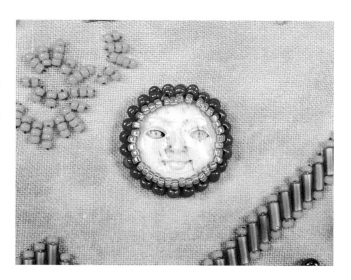

The method for beading a bezel shown below is quite flexible, allowing the bezel to be any shape (round, oval, angular), any height, and even variable height to accommodate a cabochon that is higher on one side than the other. Similar to making barnacles (see page 171), it requires circling the cabochon with tall stacks and then joining the top beads of the stacks to gather them together. This makes the stacks slant inward around the cabochon, which holds it in place on the beading surface.

1 **Preparing the Cabochon**
   Temporarily stitch the cabochon in place using a new thread. Hold the cabochon in position with your nondominant hand, and stitch to the surface next to it.

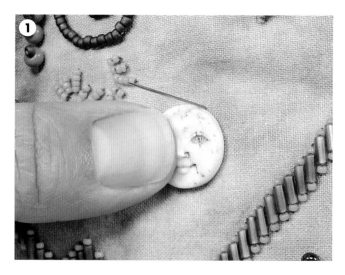

2 Cross over the top of the cabochon, and stitch to the back.

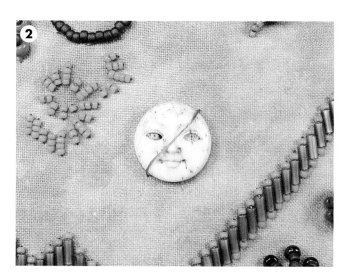

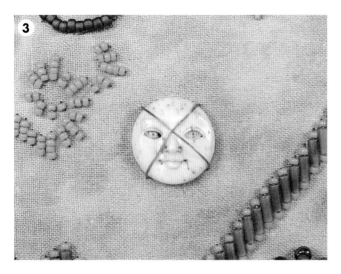

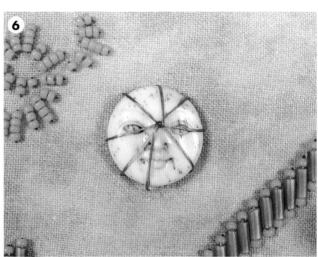

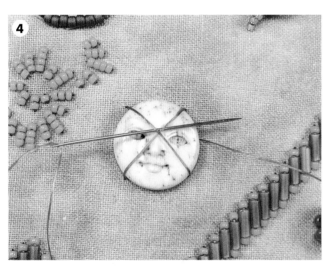

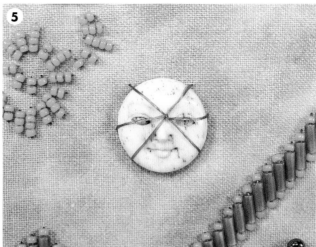

3 Stitch to the surface one-fourth of the way around the cabochon. Cross over the top of it, and stitch to the back.

4 Stitch to the surface midway between two threads. With the needle pointing to where the thread exits, stitch under the two crossed threads on top of the cabochon.

5 Pull snug, and stitch to the back on the opposite side of the cabochon.

6 Repeat steps 4–5 around the cabochon until it is securely fastened to the beading surface. Knot on the back, and snip the thread. These stitches are temporary. They will be removed after the bezel is complete.

7 Beading the Bezel

Start with a new thread about 3' (91.4 cm) long. Stitch to the surface next to the cabochon. Make a tall stack (see page 148) using size-11 beads for the trunk and a size-15 bead at the top.

The height of the stack is important. If the stacks are too high, they will cover too much of the cabochon. If they are too low, the cabochon might slip out of the bezel. Looking at the cabochon in profile, the stacks should be one bead taller than where the cabochon slants noticeably inward. Most cabochons require stacks that are three to five beads high.

8 Repeating step 7, make adjacent tall stacks all the way around the cabochon.

If the cabochon is uneven, one part higher than another, adjust the height of the stacks gradually to accommodate the unevenness.

9 After completing the stacks, knot on the back. Stitch to the surface, passing through the beads in the first stack and exiting at the top of the stack.

10 Stitch through the top bead of the next stack. Stitch through the top bead of every stack, all the way around, joining them together in a ring of beads.

Often it is necessary to add an extra size-15 bead between top beads in several places, especially along straighter sides of the cabochon. Periodically, while stitching through the top beads, pull the thread snug and check to see if the stacks are starting to tip to the side. If they are, add extra beads, distributed evenly along the ring of top beads.

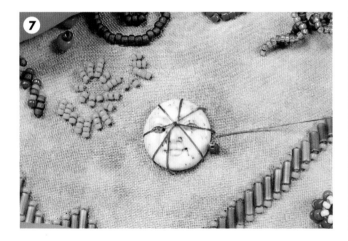

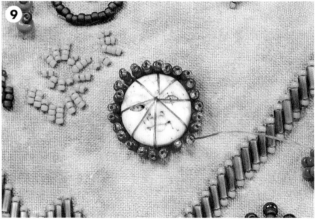

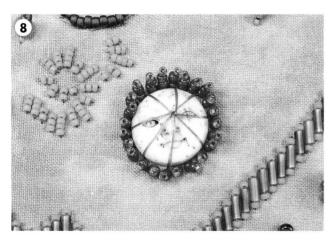

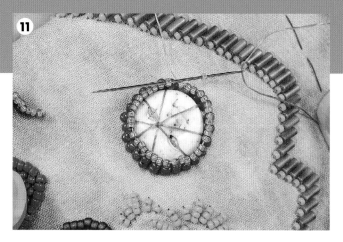

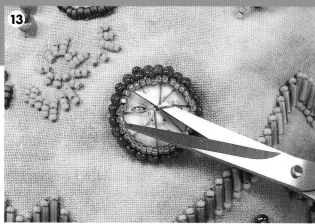

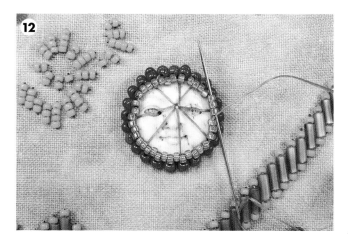

13 Snip and remove the temporary stitches holding the cabochon.

Completing the Surface Stitches

Practice and play with all the stitches to fill the surface of the sampler evenly. Some samplers are quite attractive and look good when framed.

Alternate Method for Making a Beaded Bezel

Bezels can also be made using tubular peyote stitch. First backstitch a line of size-11 beads around the perimeter of the cabochon. Then work tubular peyote stitch the same way as for the *Barnacle Brooch* (see page 90).

11 After stitching all of the way around, stitch through the top bead of the first stack a second time.

Stitch down through all the beads of the second stack to the back. Pull the thread snug from the back. Check to see if there is thread showing in the line of beads joining all of the stacks. If there is, estimate the number of beads width of thread showing and note the locations. Unthread the needle and back the thread out so that none of the stacks are joined at the top. Rejoin the top beads of the stacks, adding the estimated number of beads in the noted locations. Also check to see if the bezel seems tall enough to secure the cabochon. If not, take it out and make taller stacks.

12 When the line of beads at the top of the stacks looks right, with no thread visible, and the cabochon seems secure, knot on the back. Stitch to the surface, through one of the stacks, and sew through all of the top beads one or more times.

Sew through one of the stacks to the back, and knot.

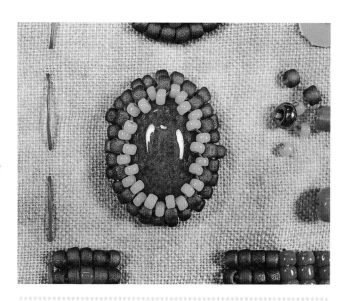

EDGE STITCHES

Bead-Embroidery Sampler

Edge stitches are used to decorate the edges of things, such as purse flaps, pendants, collars, and quilts. They are also used to embellish flat seams, to attach one piece to another, and to fasten a lining to a beaded piece. While there are many possible types of edge stitches, the three most commonly used are single bead, picot, and whipped edge stitch.

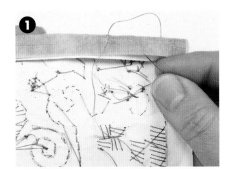

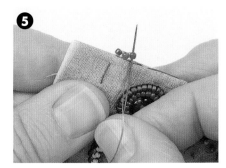

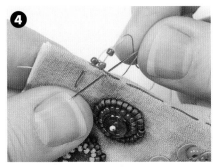

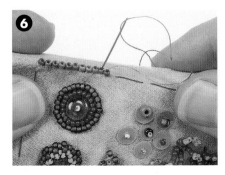

1   To practice edge stitches, fold the seam allowance at the top of the sampler to the back along the basted line. Work with size-11 beads. Stitch to the surface at the top left corner of the sampler.

2   **Single-Bead Edge Stitch**
String two beads. Stitch across the fold line from back to front, one bead's width away from the starting point.

3   Stitch through the second bead from the underside, close to the fabric, upward.

4   String one bead. Stitch across the fold line from back to front, one bead's width away from the previous stitch.

5   Stitch through the bead just added from the underside, close to the fabric, upward.

Repeat steps 4–5 several times. Note that the beads touch each other and that the thread shows along the top edge.

6   To end, after step 5, stitch back down through the second to the last bead to the underside of the fold, and knot.

8 Looking at the beads gathered in step 2, ask yourself, "What if I wanted to put something in one of the blank areas? What might it be?" As soon as your attention settles on something, pick it up and sew it on your piece. Play with the area around it, adding more beads, perhaps beading the background around it, or perhaps allowing the fabric to show.

9 Repeat the process and the question in step 8 until all of the areas are pleasing to your eye and complete. Often there are certain motifs, such as the burgundy flowers or the little pink-centered scallops, that are fun to do. Repeating those motifs in different areas provides a sense of balance and unity to the piece.

10 To finish the ATC, remove the basting stitches from around the edge, tear away the stabilizing paper around the border, and trim off the excess fabric leaving about ½" (1.3 cm) margin outside the border. Fold under the edges at the borders, miter the corners, and finger press or baste in place.

11 Cut a piece of heavy card stock to 2½" x 3½" (6.4 x 8.9 cm) or use a commercial blank ATC. Cut a piece of synthetic suede the same size for the backing. Slip the card inside the folded edges of the beaded fabric. Cover with the backing. Use any edge stitch to sew the backing to the beaded fabric. Use a permanent ink pen to write the name of the ATC, your name, and the date on the backing.

RAVEN MOON ATC

Preplanned Bead Embroidery on Stiffened Felt

This project is another beaded artist trading card, in the standard size of 2½" x 3½"(6.4 x 8.9 cm). It may be traded for one by another artist. The same techniques can be used to make larger or smaller pieces. This is a particularly good method for making brooches and pendants.

7 Changing Beading Locations

There are three methods commonly used to travel from one beading area to another some distance away (more than ¼" [6 mm]). If both locations are near a line of beads, stitch through the line of beads, exiting at the point closest to where the next bead is to be added. Stitch to the back. Stitch to the front at the new beading point.

8 The second method for changing beading locations is to sew between the layers of fabric (along the batting), exiting so the needle is positioned for the next stitch. Before adding beads, sew to the back and return to the surface, thus quilting the layers together.

9 Changing Threads

The third method to change beading locations is to knot off the thread and begin with a waste knot in the new location. To knot off the thread, sew to the back. Take a small stitch where the thread exits, catching only a few fabric threads in the stitch. Pull the thread until a small loop becomes visible. Sew through the loop one time to make an overhand knot. Optional: Sew through the loop twice to make a double knot.

10 Sew into the fabric next to the knot, and run the needle between the layers (through the batting) for about 1" (2.5 cm). Sew to the surface on the back, pull the thread slightly, and snip the thread next to the fabric.

(continued)

11 Finish Beading the Center Panel

Continue beading to complete the center panel of the piece. Work in one area at a time, switching colors of beads as required by the design. To keep the quilted surface even, space the beading evenly across the center panel of the quilt. If the design requires more beading in one area, there can be noticeable shrinkage in that area. To resolve this issue, add extra hand- or machine-quilting stitches to the other areas of the center panel.

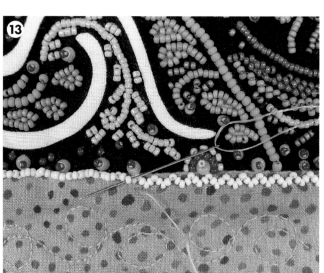

12 Beading the Inside Border

For some designs, it looks good to bead only the center panel. For others, beaded borders make an attractive "frame" around the center panel and tie the whole piece together. *For Five Cats in the Yard,* a picot-edge stitch is added around the center panel to quilt the seam and to pull the white color outward. This picot stitch is worked the same way as shown on page 177, except that it begins with five beads, and four beads are added with each stitch afterward. The spacing between each stitch is about three bead's width.

13 Edge stitches worked along the seam will tend to "stand upright." To make the points lie flat, quilt through all layers along the edge about ¼" (6 mm) from the seam. Catch the center bead of a point with each stitch.

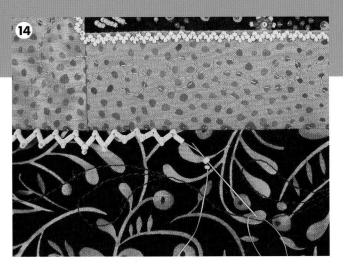

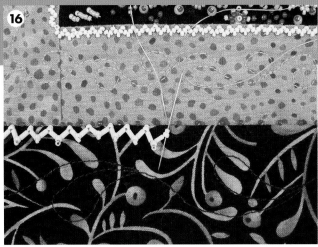

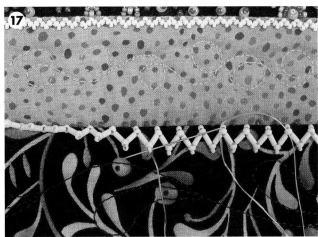

14 Beading the Outer Border

Quilt in the ditch along the seam line around the outer border. Add a bead to each stitch, spacing the beads at ¼" (6 mm) intervals. This provides seam quilting as well as a spacing guide for the bugle-bead edge stitch.

For the bugle-bead edge stitch, one unit = one bugle bead, one size-11 seed bead, and one size-15 seed bead, strung in that order. Starting in one corner, string one size-15 bead, one size-11 bead, and one unit. Slide the beads to the quilt surface. Skipping the last bead, sew back through the size-11 bead toward the seam. Pull it snug.

15 String one unit. Stitch through the edge of the seam about ¼" (6 mm) from the starting point, midway between two of the spacer beads. Do not sew to the back of the quilt with this stitch. Catch only a few threads in the outside border, exiting at the seam.

16 Sew back through the size-11 bead toward the outside edge of the quilt. Pull it snug. This completes one point. Continue all the way around the border, repeating steps 14–16. String one unit for each step.

17 To make the edging lie flat, quilt along the edge about ⅜" (1 cm) from the seam. Catch the center bead of a point with each stitch. Optional: Embellish the corners with flower and leaf beads.

Finishing: Remove the basting stitches. Trim the batting and back flush with the top, squaring up the sides if necessary. Use standard quilting methods to attach the binding. If desired, add a sleeved hanging-dowel and signature patch to the back of the quilt.

LITTLE ME

Beaded Doll

Make a beaded cloth doll or embellish a stuffed animal with beads as a special keepsake or gift.

Use any of the bead-embroidery stitches and techniques, especially seed, fringing, and edge stitches. The only limitation with this project is that it's not possible to sew to the back of the fabric once the doll is made. For that reason, a few different stitching methods are shown.

This doll needs a face, which can be either a carved cabochon (bone, polymer clay, or other material) or a picture printed on fabric. When selecting fabric, beads, and ephemera for the *Little Me* doll, choose items that have special meaning.

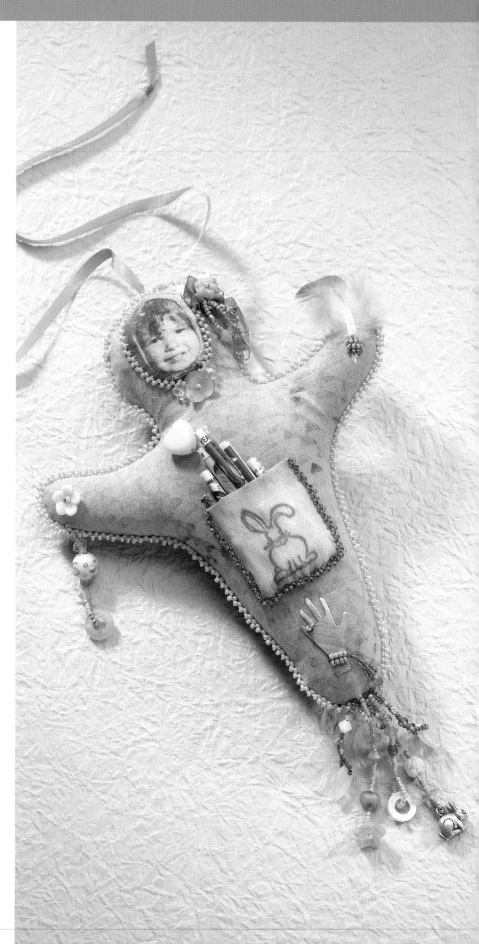

YOU WILL NEED

- one piece of fabric for front of doll, approximately 8" (20.3 cm) square

- one piece of fabric for back of doll, approximately 8" (20.3 cm) square (can be same fabric as front)

- one face image on inkjet printable fabric (or a face cabochon, or a face cut from commercial fabric)

- one wad of stuffing (for pillows, toys, dolls), cotton, polyester, or wool

- short beading needle, size 11 or 10

- beading thread, Nymo or equivalent, size D, color: neutral or same as backing fabric

- 5–15 g assorted seed beads, various colors and sizes

- assorted embellishments (accent beads, charms, feather, key, lace, ribbons, etc.)

- 16" (40.6 cm) ribbon, narrow (for ties, optional)

1   Making the Doll

Make a paper pattern for an original doll shape, or enlarge and trace a pattern from the photograph above. Layer the two pieces of fabric, right sides together, and pin the pattern to the fabric. Cut out the doll. Using a very small running stitch, hand sew around the doll about ⅛" (3 mm) from the edge. Leave a 2" (5 cm) opening along one side. Clip the curves. Turn the doll right side out. Using very small puffs of stuffing, stuff the head first, then the arms, and finally the body. The doll should feel firm, but not rigid. Whip stitch the opening closed.

Print the image of a face, perhaps a childhood picture, following the instructions on a package of inkjet-printable fabric. Cut out the face leaving a ¼" (6 mm) margin. Turn under the margin, and finger press. Use the picot edge stitch (see page 177) to bead around the face.

(continued)

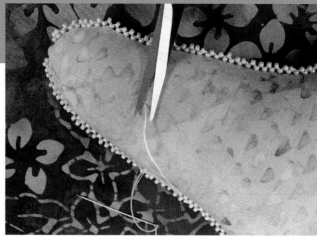

2 Waste Knot

To begin beading on the doll, make a waste knot. Use a single thread, knotted at the end. Insert the needle about 1" (2.5 cm) from where the first bead will be added. Stitch through the doll's body, and exit at the point where the beading will start. Take a tiny stitch at the exit point. Pull the thread until a small loop appears. Stitch through the loop twice. Slowly pull the knot tight. Pull the original (waste) knot away from the doll's body, and snip it off.

To conceal and reinforce the seam, make a picot edge stitch around the doll. To avoid a crowded look at the neck and arm curves, increase the spacing between stitches slightly in these areas. Leave a small open space at the bottom of the doll, where fringes will be attached later.

3 Knotting Off

Finish by making a small stitch next to or under the last bead. Pull the thread until a small loop appears. Sew through the loop twice, and slowly pull the knot tight. Insert the needle into the doll's body right next to the knot, and exit about 1" (2.5 cm) away. Snip the thread.

4 Attach the Face

Pin the face in place. Make a waste knot (step 2), and prepare to sew at one of the points in the edge stitch around the face. Sew around the face with a small running stitch, catching a point in each stitch. Knot off (step 3). If the face is a cabochon, attach it using a beaded bezel (see page 172).

5 Use ribbon scraps, lace, and beads to make a head ornament. Stitch it in place.

6 Decorate the body of the doll with beads and other ephemera. For each beaded area, begin with a waste knot, and bury the tail after knotting off. Travel from one beading area to an adjacent area by stitching through the doll's body to the new area.

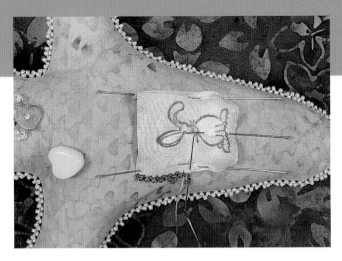
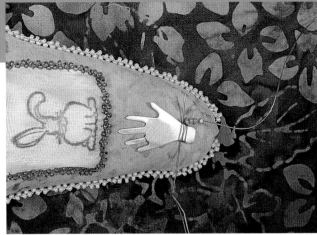

7 Add a Pocket

One way to add items that have no hole is to make a pocket for them. Double a scrap of ribbon, tucking in the ends, and sew it to the doll's body as a pocket. This doll's ribbon pocket, decorated with rubber stamping, holds rolled-up postage stamps, each symbolizing something significant.

8 Attach an Item with No Hole

Attach an item with no hole, such as the hand, by couching over the top of it with thread. Then hide the stitches with beaded lazy stitch (see page 151).

9 Attach a Feather

To attach a feather, first snip away the downy barbs from the lower quill. Couch the feather to the doll by stitching over the stripped part of the quill. When the feather is secure, hide the stitches with beaded lazy stich as in step 8.

10 Add fringes (see page 179) to the arm and bottom of the doll. This is also a good way to add charms and special beads.

Optional: To display the doll suspended from a cupboard knob, mirror, or lamp, sew the middle of a 16" (40.5 cm) length of ribbon to the top of the doll's head.

BEADED GREETING CARD

Beading on Paper

Enjoy an hour or two embellishing a mixed-media collage on paper with sparkling, three-dimensional bead embroidery. This is a lovely way to feature special or vintage beads, highlight a collage or photograph, add three-dimensional elements to artwork, or enhance a purchased greeting card.

Sewing beads on paper enables you to attach them invisibly and neatly, providing a stronger and more accurate fastening method than glue. Unlike beading on cloth, the holes for the beads must be pierced before sewing on the beads.

While the illustrated project is a greeting card, the same methods apply to beading any heavy, stiff paper to create art of any size. High-quality cotton or linen rag paper is recommended for strong paper structure and longevity of the work. Suggested papers include 140-lb. to 300-lb. watercolor paper, handmade papers, card-stock, and purchased artist trading cards.

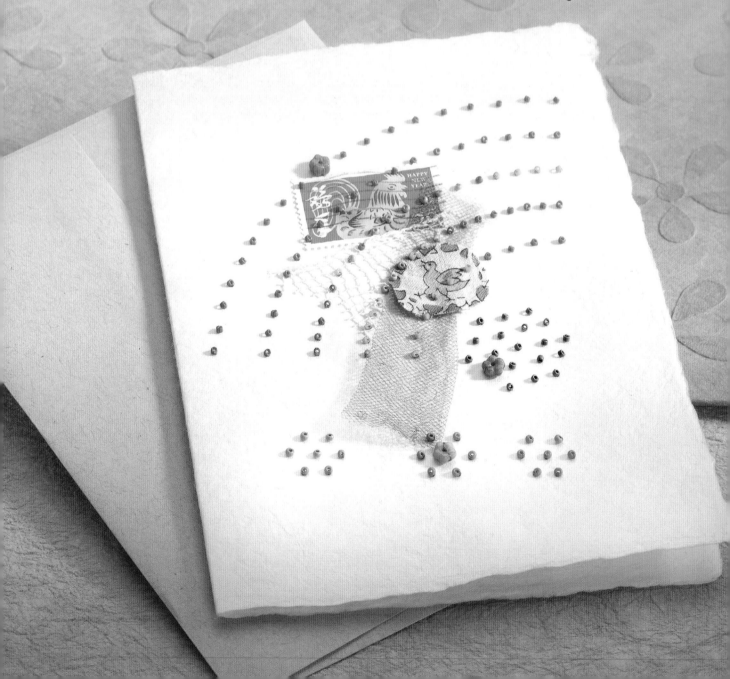

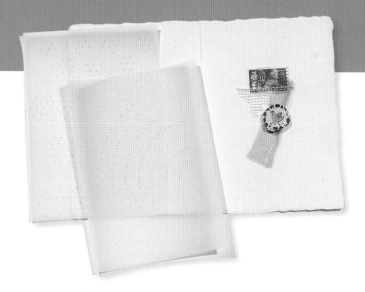

YOU WILL NEED

- blank greeting card of heavy, stiff paper or cardstock

- glue stick, permanent bond

- tracing vellum (thick, smooth tracing paper)

- push pin, T-pin or bookbinder's needle tool

- ¼" (6 mm) foam core board or heavy corrugated cardboard, a few inches (centimeters) larger than project

- mat board or cutting mat to protect the table while piercing holes

- assorted collage elements such as postage stamps, decorative papers, ribbon, fabric scraps

- assorted seed beads, any size

- optional: sequins, buttons, charms (lightweight, flat elements work well)

- beading needle, size 10 or 11

- beading thread, Nymo or equivalent, size D

1 Choose a commercial, blank card or make one from stiff, heavy cardstock. Deckle edges or decorative inclusions in the paper add to the overall design. Select and arrange collage elements on the front of the card in a pleasing design. Plan the arrangement of beads, where they will go in the design, and how they will relate to the collage.

Beads of different sizes and shapes will orient themselves differently on the paper. To see what various beads and pattern arrangements will look like, sew a variety of beads on an extra piece of paper as a sampler.

2 Piercing holes is a commitment because they can't be undone. The only way to hide a hole in paper is to sew a bead there. To embroider a planned arrangement or repeating pattern of beads on the card, first create a template by drawing or tracing a pattern of dots on smooth vellum tracing paper. To make an evenly spaced pattern, mark intersections on graph paper with dots. Then place vellum over the graph paper and use a fine-tip pen with permanent, non-smearing ink to trace the dot pattern on the vellum. The dots should be placed at least ¹⁄₁₆" (1.6 mm) apart.

(continued)

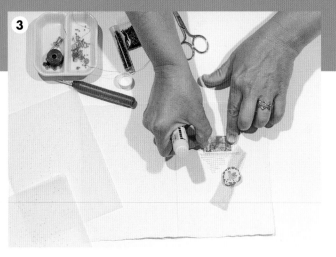

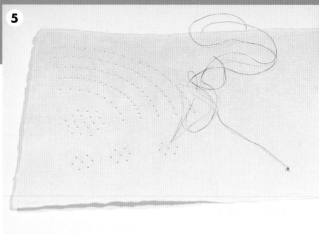

3 Use a glue stick to tack the collage elements on the front of the card, which will hold them in place while beading. Only a minimal amount of glue is needed, because the beads sewn through the collage elements will further fasten them to the paper. Do not use rubber cement, double-stick tape, or plastic adhesives, as these will gum up the piercing pin, beading needle, and thread. If the collage begins to buckle slightly, use a book or other weight to press the collage while the glue dries. Allow the glue to dry fully before beginning the next step.

4 Make a layered stack on the worktable with the mat board on the bottom, the foam core in the middle, and the card, faceup, on top. Align the vellum template over the collage. Use a push-pin, T-pin, or needle tool to pierce holes through the card at each spot where you plan to place a bead. To pierce a large or complex design, it will help to temporarily fasten the card and template to the foam core with removable tape.

5 To sew seed beads on the card, use a single thread. Although the thread will be barely visible, choose a color to match the beads or perhaps one to provide a little contrast. Tie a knot at the end that is large enough to avoid slipping through the hole in the paper.

6 Starting on the back, push the needle up through the first hole at one edge of the design. Tug gently on the thread to be sure the knot on the back holds. Pick up a bead on the needle and slide it down almost to the paper. Put the needle back into the same hole. Pull the thread from below to attach the bead snugly against the paper.

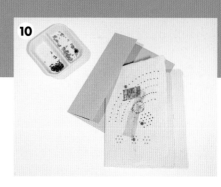

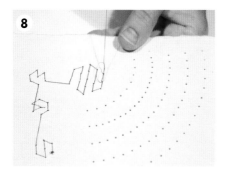

9 If needed, pierce additional holes to add more beads to the design or to add stabilizing stitches to a larger element. Buttons and/or larger beads may be added after sewing the seed beads in place. Some larger buttons may require larger holes in the paper and thicker thread. Place larger holes at least ⅛" (3 mm) apart. To support heavier elements, choose extra-heavyweight paper in the design stage.

10 When the beading is finished, protect and hide the threads by gluing a piece of lightweight decorative paper to the inside of the card. Or, it may be fun to see the patterns made by the thread on the inside. If so, protect the threads with a piece of tracing vellum. To send the card through the postal system, shield the beads with a double layer of tissue or a piece of thin mailing foam.

7 From the back, put the needle up through the next hole, pick up a bead, slide it down, put the needle back through the same hole, and pull the thread from below to set the bead tight. Continue working your way through the design from one hole to the next hole until every hole is filled or until the thread gets short.

8 To tie off a thread on the back of the paper, make several half-hitches around the thread between the last two holes. Cut the remaining thread, leaving a ½" (1.3 cm) tail.

Variations

Use these same methods to create wall art. To make a piece larger than 4" x 5" (10 x 13 cm), 300-lb. paper is recommended. For pieces larger than 12" (30.5 cm), precut artist's stretcher bars can be used as a temporary frame to support the edges of the paper while working. If you frame the work behind glass, use a mat or spacers to keep the beads from touching the glass.

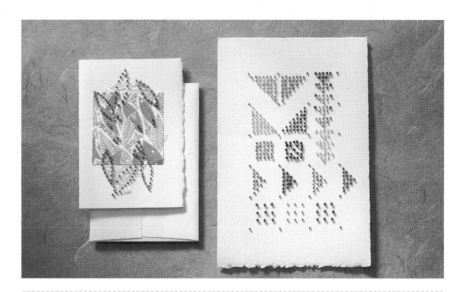

MIXED METHODS

So far in this book, each project features a single technique. However, beaders often combine two or more techniques to create complex projects. For example, it is common for bead weavers to combine several methods of bead weaving, especially when creating three-dimensional pieces.

Bead embroidery also lends itself to a mixed-method approach. Serenity is one of many ways to combine bead embroidery with bead weaving. *Summer Rain* illustrates a method for working bead embroidery into a fiber-art wall hanging. As beaders experiment more and more with mixed methods of beading, the creative scope of beadwork expands significantly.

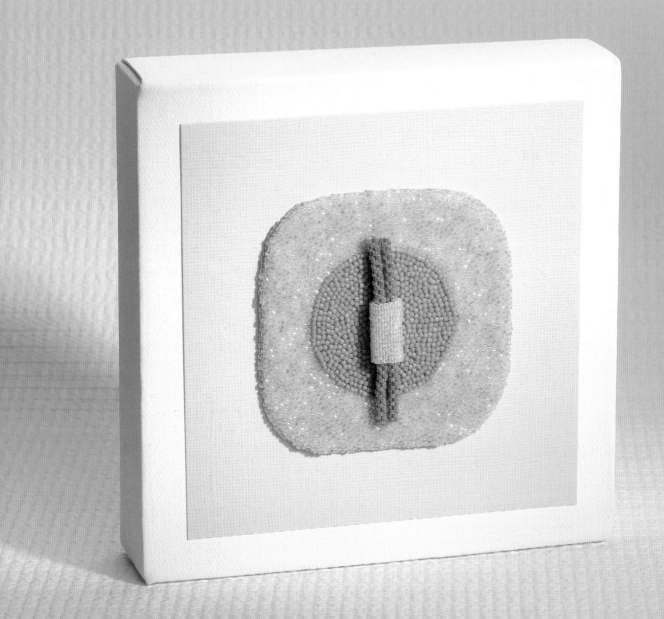

SUMMER RAIN, A STORY CLOTH

Bead Embroidery and Fiber Arts

Create a bead-embroidered story cloth and discover a meaningful way to tell a personal story by combining the colors and textures of recycled fabrics with the beauty of beads. The story can record a memory or capture a feeling. It can be autobiographical—depicting a special life moment, perhaps even a dream—or loosely interpret the essence of a season, or the depth of an emotion. While the example is all about "summer rain," you are encouraged to tell your own story using the combined methods of fiber arts and bead embroidery.

The story begins with recycled scraps of fabric, woven together to form a base cloth for beadwork and other embellishments. Repurposing fabric in this way can be integral to the story itself. For example, using a piece of lace from your grandmother's hankie or remnants from a loved one's old, worn work shirt can bring special meaning to a story cloth about a particular person. Similarly, a piece of vintage velvet can contribute to a mood or feeling, and torn bits from a well-used linen hand towel might evoke a history of purpose and intention. Consider the previous life of various textiles. Choose the fabrics, beads, and embellishments with these thoughts in mind.

This kind of storytelling is an excellent way to experiment with new techniques and materials since there are no hard and fast rules. Improvisation is the compass.

YOU WILL NEED

Assorted fabric scraps: torn remnants with frayed edges, odd and irregular shapes including leftover pieces from previous projects, all work well. Mixing fabrics with different textures (such as linen, silk, velvet, and cottons) adds interest.

- assorted embroidery threads
- embroidery needle
- small sharp scissors
- assorted beads: seed beads (size 8, 11, 13 charlottes, and 15), bugle beads, and shaped glass beads (such as leaves and squares)
- beading needles appropriate for the sizes of beads you are using
- beading thread: Nymo or equivalent, size D

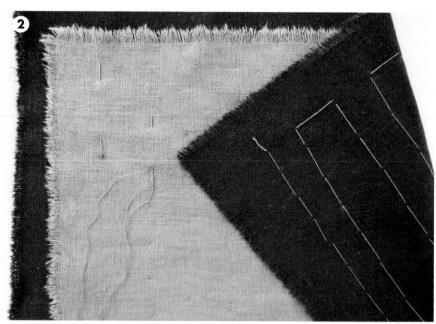

1 Choose an overall size and a color palette for the story, and then gather a pile of fabric scraps in various shapes and sizes. Having more fabric on hand than needed makes assembling the base cloth easier. Different textures (such as linen, silk, and velvet), prints, and patterns add visual interest.

Deliberately fray the edges by tearing the fabrics or pulling threads on cut edges. Tear some narrow strips. Then wash all the fabrics in the washing machine and dry them in a hot dryer. This will further fray and fluff the edges. Plus, more important, after machine washing, the edges will be stabilized, not fraying further. Hand washing may be necessary for very delicate materials. Iron each scrap. Flat pieces are easier to layer and hand stitch.

2 To prepare the base cloth foundation, pin two pieces of fabric together, the smaller piece on top. With a single strand of embroidery floss in a matching color, sew them together. Use an invisible basting stitch, making a large stitch on the back side and a very tiny stitch on the front. It is essential that these two fabrics are securely fastened together.

3 Lay various scraps on the base cloth and move them around until you achieve a pleasing arrangement. Pin them in place. Begin weaving some pieces together (smaller scraps are good for this). Tear larger scraps to form "fingers" to weave through.

4 Continue weaving the scraps until the surface is covered. Longer pieces can extend over the edge. Vary the weaving to add interest, allowing some edges to show, some to disappear. Also, stack fabric (thin over thick) to add variation. Some fabrics fray beautifully and make excellent borders or fringes for the bottom edge of the piece.

5 Use invisible basting stitches to sew the woven strips to the base cloth. In areas where the fabric is stacked, be sure to baste securely around the edges of the top fabric as well. Cut off any "tails" that extend past the base cloth, fray the new edges, and baste in place.

6 Using two strands of embroidery floss, add decorative embroidery stitches. A simple wrap stitch (or satin stitch) gives a highly visual effect. There are countless other embroidery stitches that might be fun as well. Variegated embroidery floss offers more visual dimension than monocolored floss.

7 Choose narrow fabric strips and fold and/or twist them into lines. Pin them on the base cloth. Use a double strand of embroidery floss and wrap the line with stitches, couching them in place. The wrapping threads can be evenly spaced or varied.

(continued)

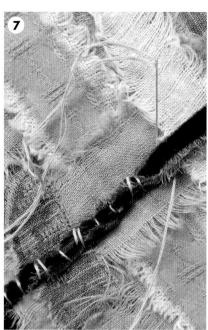

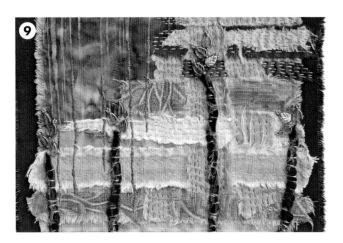

8 Use two strands of embroidery floss and add irregular running stitches. Vary the floss colors and the sewing directions. Sew past the ends of some of the fabric strips for visual interest. Leave some strips unstitched, if you prefer. This is a good time to add bits of fabric to areas that need it.

9 Begin beading by attaching the larger beads first. This helps to set the overall balance of the piece. Secure larger beads by going back and forth through the bead at least twice.

10 Bead two ruffles (page 170), side by side, using size-11 seed beads. Choose a dark color for the stacks and top each stack with a lighter color bead. Join the top beads by using a mix of beads within the same lighter color range.

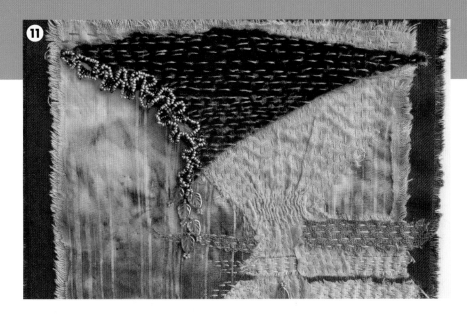

11 Feel your way through the process of surface embellishment, alternating stitching with beading to keep the work both pleasing and true to the story. Beads have a strong visual impact. Thus, as more beads are added, other areas may require more embroidery detail. Work with these areas until they feel balanced.

12 Add motion to vertical spaces by beading wavy lines. In this example, lines of long, twisted bugle beads mixed with short bugle beads and seed beads create the sense of rain. And short stacks made with size-6 seed beads topped with size-13 faceted seed beads create the impression of raindrops.

13 Attach shaped beads, such as the square beads on the example. Bead around each shaped bead twice with size-15 seed beads.

Continue adding beads and thread embroidery, until you sense that the story cloth is complete.

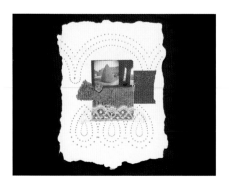

Carol Berry
Bellingham, WA

www.BrowerandBerry.com

Carol makes paper, weaves cloth, and collects lost gloves, rusted metal, bottle caps, buttons, cloth fragments, beads, stamps, and pieces of string. Her assembled collages are pierced and embroidered with hundreds of minute glass beads. She has been sewing and beading for over fifty years. Project by Carol Berry: *Beaded Greeting Card* (page 204).

Christi Carter
Lopez Island, WA

http://sweetpeapath.blogspot.com

Christi began beading on cloth during the Bead Journal Project, 2007. Since then, telling stories with bead embroidery and layered fabrics has become her passion. Her pieces are all hand stitched, using reclaimed textiles. Christi is also a photographer and a member of the Surface Design Association. Project by Christi Carter: *Summer Rain Story Cloth* (page 212).

Clarissa Ceruti
Thousand Oaks, CA

www.etsy.com/shop/Clarissa68
http://1000quercenews.wordpress.com

Clarissa, a scientist during the day and an artist at night, became intrigued by crocheting with beads in 2004 after seeing another artist's work. She enjoys making necklaces, bracelets, and small accessories, such as phone charms and key chains. She sells her beadwork through Etsy and consignment stores. Project by Clarissa Ceruti: *Polka-Dot Bracelet* (page 123).

Lisa Criswell
Scottsdale, AZ

indigosbeads@live.com

Lisa's bead journey began in 2006 with designing tapestry pieces, which she wove on a loom or with square stitch. She developed and sold patterns for her tapestries. Two years later, a new world of beading opened to Lisa as she began experimenting with bead embroidery. Her active mind and skilled hands are always seeking new ways to create with beads. Projects by Lisa Criswell: *Autumn Crystals Belt* (page 96) and *Summer Breeze Bracelet* (page 110).

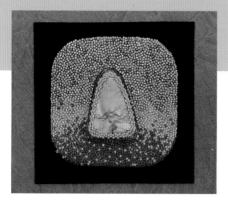

Denise Dineen
GA and ME

www.estsy.com/shop/atlanticneedlearts
www.atlanticneedlearts.wordpress.com

Denise began beading in 1994. Prior to the Bead Journal Project, her primary focus was designing holiday ornaments worked in peyote stitch. Since then, journaling through bead embroidery has become her passion. Denise is also a calligrapher and a juried member of the League of New Hampshire Craftsmen. Projects by Denise Dineen: *Vermillion Heart Pin* (page 100) and *Serenity* (page 208).

Ann Severine
Santa Fe, NM

www.annseverine.com

After her first beading class in 1991, Ann felt like Alice falling down the rabbit hole. From childhood, she knitted, crocheted, embroidered, and sewed, always using patterns. With beads she is now free of this dependence on the work of others, experiencing the joy of creativity and teaching. Project by Ann Severine: *Saraguro Lace Collar* (page 118).

Marcie Stone
Portland, OR

www.hanson-stone.com
www.hansonstonehandmade.etsy.com

Marcie's passion for beading began in the early 1980s when she used beads to embellish her pine-needle baskets. This evolved into sculptural seed-bead work, which is central to her creative process. Fascinated by the way the different beads play against each other, Marcie creates jeweled encrustations influenced by organic forms. Project by Marcie Stone: *Barnacle Brooch* (page 90).

Sylvia Windhurst
Richmond, RI

www.windyriver.etsy.com
http://windyriver.blogspot.com

After years of working as a graphic artist, Sylvia reconnected with handwork, revisiting her previous passions for beading and embroidery. She particularly enjoys bead embroidery and off-loom bead weaving. Many of her pieces combine those two techniques, along with surface or crewel embroidery. Project by Sylvia Windhurst: *Fan Earrings* (page 104).

Rochelle Zawisza
Henderson, NV

www.justbeads.wordpress.com
www.flickr.com/photos/justbeads
justbeads@ymail.com

Rochelle's fascination with beading began with a Mill Hill Christmas Ornament kit in 1990. Although she has since learned many complex techniques and projects, her passion centers around making holiday-themed items using peyote stitch with Delicas and Swarovski crystals. Projects by Rochelle Zawisza: *Stocking Ornament* (page 82) and *Miniature Basket* (page 86).

RESOURCE LIST

The sources listed below are recommended by the author and contributors to this book as friendly, reliable retailers that offer a wide selection of quality beads and beading supplies. Each of them accepts major credit cards and overseas orders.

Fusion Beads

Seattle, WA
store: 206-782-4595
online: 888-781-3559
FusionBeads.com
info@fusionbeads.com

Excellent online source for all beading needs; inspiring selection of seed beads with color-accurate pictures and sort-by-color feature; quality tools and supplies; volume discounts; easily navigated website; easy to order. Note: Thanks to Fusion Beads for providing images of tools and supplies for this book.

Out on a Whim

Cotati, CA
707-664-8343
800-232-3111
www.whimbeads.com
info@whimbeads.com

Wonderful source! Japanese seed beads in all sizes, shapes, and colors with color-accurate pictures, sort-by-bead-finish feature, and easily navigated website; Swarovski crystal elements; pressed glass beads, chain, findings, beading tools, and supplies.

Beadcats

Wilsonville, OR
503-625-2323
www.beadcats.com
orders@beadcats.com

Great selection of Czech pressed-glass beads (leaves, flowers, drops, pendants, etc.) in many unusual colors; Japanese seed beads (cubes, triangles, hexcuts, tilas, peanuts, cylinders); vintage seed beads (size 16 to 24); needles and threads, beading supplies. Color-matching services.

Storm Cloud Trading

St. Paul, MN
651-645-0343
www.beadstorm.com
BeadStorm1@aol.com

Twenty-five years in business! Great selection of seed beads, Swarovski crystal elements, pressed glass, stone beads, leather, and beading supplies. If it's not on the website, call or email—they probably have it.

Beyond Beadery

Rollinsville, CO
800-840-5548
866-FAX-BEAD
www.beyondbeadery.com
info@beyondbeadery.com

In business since 1987! Excellent selection of seed beads in all sizes, shapes, and colors; other fun stuff.

Caravan Beads

Portland, ME
207-761-2503
800-230-8941
fax: 207-874-2664
www.caravanbeads.net
barryk@caravanbeads.net

Large selection of seed beads, crystals, strands, stringing materials, Ultrasuede, bead design software.

Joggles.com, LLC

West Warwick, RI
401-615-7696
www.joggles.com
barbara@joggles.com

Wide selection of materials and supplies for mixed-media artists; beads, embellishments, fibers and threads, dyes, paint, ribbons, buttons, patterns, journals, wool felt, etc.

ACKNOWLEDGMENTS

Thank you to the team at Creative Publishing international for the opportunity to write the book my students and colleagues have wanted for the past thirty years! This is the book I wished was available when I started beading in 1985, a time when there was not a single book about beading in print. Today, among thousands of current bead-related books, this one stands alone as an in-depth, comprehensive guide to beads and all types of beading. I am honored to have the opportunity to share with you what took me three decades to learn.

Special thanks to my husband, Robert Demar! I could not have given eight solid months of time to this book without his easygoing, generous advocacy.

Thank you to my guest artists and other beady friends, who have encouraged me and contributed their time and talents to these pages. Thank you to Lisa Criswell, Christi Carter, Lunnette Higdon-Hertel, Thom Atkins, Liz Chenoweth, Gayle Hazelton, and Janet Dann for their suggestions and unceasing support. Thank you to Christy Hinkle, Leah Altman, and Lunette Higdon-Hertel whose capable hands you see in the photographs.

Thank you also to Lindsay Burke and her team at Fusion Beads for providing quality photographs of beading tools and supplies.

ABOUT THE AUTHOR

Robin Atkins is an internationally known bead artist, instructor, author, and speaker. Her beadwork includes framed, sculptural, and wearable pieces. A studio artist since 1985, she enjoys all types of beading, but her greatest passion is bead embroidery.

Robin is author of and contributing artist to numerous books and magazine articles, and founder of The Bead Journal Project. She teaches at national conferences and for guilds around the country. The primary focus in Robin's books and workshops is the exploration of creativity and the development of personal style. She is also known for her research and knowledge about the history of beads and bead-making technology.

website: www.robinatkins.com
blog: http://beadlust.blogspot.com

Index